# 100ʊ Columbo Facts

Phillip Alan

# Contents

# Introduction

Columbo is an iconic police procedural show which ran from 1968 to 2003. The show was very popular during its run, especially in the 1970s and remains very popular today throughout the world.

The show has a wonderful performance by Peter Falk as the disheveled, eccentric but extremely able detective. The world depicted is colourful and often surreal with Columbo chasing murderers who are often rich and highly intelligent. Columbo has high production values, great writing, wonderful guest stars and many famous personalities involved in production.

Find out more about the world of Columbo with this book with information on the cast and crew, anecdotes, episodes, characters, locations, mistakes and other fascinating Columbo facts in this book.

# The Facts

**1**

In Candidate for Crime (1973) the shadows of the microphone/boom can be shown on the front door when Mrs Haywood lets Columbo in for the first time.

**2**

Ed Asner was going to be cast as Colonel Rumford in By Dawn's Early Light? (1974) but he pulled out. Patrick McGoohan took the role.

**3**

Peter Falk was a fan of the tune This Old Man and whistled it during filming Any Old Port in a Storm (1973) as an ad-lib. It became a part of the series and Columbo's theme tune.

**4**

In 2013 a Writers Guild of America list of the 101 Best Written TV Series included Columbo at 57.

**5**

The initial pilot episode of Columbo, titled Prescription: Murder, aired on February 20th 1968. The final installment of Columbo, titled Columbo Likes the Nightlife aired January 30th 2003. The show spanned 34 years.

**6**

In Butterfly in Shades of Grey (1994) Fielding Chase's mansion was located at 3469 Cross Creek Rd, Malibu, California, USA. The house was built in 1983 by Linda Thompson. It had nine bedrooms and eleven bathrooms. A railway linked the garden and house. The house changed hands several times since it was built and the site has been extensively renovated with the railway removed.

## 7

The quickest murder in the series is in Suitable for Framing (1971) occurring only about a minute into the episode.

## 8

Suitable for Framing (1971) has the only murder victim with no lines of dialogue.

## 9

In A Friend in Deed (1974) and Undercover (1994) the first murders occur before the episode begins.

## 10

In 1999, TV Guide magazine ranked Lt. Columbo No. 7 on a 50 Greatest TV Characters of All Time poll.

## 11

Only 504 of Columbo's Peugeot 403 Cabriolet convertible car were made in 1959.

## 12

Peter Falk enjoyed the running gag in Now You see Him

(1976) in which Columbo's wife had bought him a new raincoat which Columbo dislked. Columbo kept unsuccessfully trying to lose it.

## 13

In Old Fashioned Murder (1976) the Lytton Museum is located at Mount St. Mary's College, Doheny Mansion - 10 Chester Pl, Los Angeles, California, USA.

## 14

In a A Friend in Deed (1974) there was this interesting conversation about Columbo's vintage Peugeot car:

"Charlie Shoup (used car salesman): Yes, indeed. It's a real honey. You know we   don't get to see many of these around anymore - especially in this condition.

Columbo: Well, I try to take good care of it."

## 15

Columbo normally drinks coffee black and strong. On occasion he drinks it with cream (milk).

## 16

For the second season of Columbo executives at NBC thought it would be a good idea to give Columbo a sidekick. Columbo creators Richard Levinson and William Link had the idea of a dog as a sidekick.

Peter Falk chose the basset hound at a dog pound.

**17**

The Carsini Winery in Any Old Port in a Storm is the Mirassou Winery in real life. This is situated at Mirassou Winery, 3000 Aborn Road, San Jose, California, USA.

**18**

For the role of Negative Reaction (1974) Omar Shariff was asked to play murderer Paul Galesko. But Shariff wanted the huge fee of $100,000! Dick Van Dyke played the role.

**19**

In Mind Over Mayhem the boy genius is called Stephen Spelberg. This is a tribute by episode writers Steven Bochco and Dean Hargrove to Steven Spielberg who directed Murder by the Book in 1971.

**20**

In Uneasy Lies the Crown (1990) Colombo states that he is cold as his coat "does not have a lining"!

**21**

The background music in the jewelry store in A Friend in Deed (1974) is "The End of a Love Affair" by Edward Redding.

**22**

John Finnegan (1926-2012) was a character actor who made thirteen appearances in the Columbo series. He appears in more episodes than any other of the supporting cast.

He had a wide variety of roles from Season One's Blueprint

For Murder (1971) to the last episode Columbo likes the Nightlife in 2003. He played various characters such as a workman and garbage collector. He had several parts as a police chief. In later Columbo's he played Barney of Barney's Beanery where Columbo ate his chilli.

He became close friends with Peter Falk at the Actors Studio in his native New York City.

## 23

The children's song "This Old Man" appears in almost every episode of the Columbo series, sometimes as background music, but most often with Lt. Columbo singing, humming, or whistling the tune. Candidate For Crime (1973) is the only episode where the murderer (Jackie Cooper as political candidate Nelson Hayward) is heard using it; in this case, he is whistling it as he prepares to film a campaign commercial.

## 24

Columbo's creators decided to not have Columbo at police headquarters at home when creating the series as "it seemed to us much more effective if he drifted into our stories from limbo."

Columbo was shown at police headquarters on occasion but we never see his home - or wife.

## 25

In season one of Columbo Peter Falk used his influence on casting tried to get bit parts for his actor friends such as Mike Lally. As the series progressed he realised that guest actors had an influence on the reputation of the show and his own performance. Falk therefore asked for big names to guest star in the series.

**26**

Show creators Richard Levinson and William Link stated that they did not give Columbo a first name and did not intend for him to have one. In the first script of season one a reference to Columbo's first name was removed by them.

.

**27**

Columbo is a fan of British fish and chips. In Dagger Of The Mind (1973), Columbo says to Supt. Durk by the Embankment in London: "Those fish and chips are greasy but they're sure good!"

**28**

Columbo creator Richard Levinson stated that Columbo's "one more thing" catchphrase was invented when he and William Link wrote the original stage play. A scene was too short and Columbo had exited the stage too early. Having him say "one more thing" was an easy way to get him back on state without having to rewrite lots of dialogue.

**29**

In the 1991 episode Death Hits the Jackpot (1991), Columbo reveals that he and his wife's silver wedding anniversary - 25th - is "coming up very soon". This would mean that Columbo married two years before the 1968 pilot Prescription: Murder.

**30**

A Trace of Murder (1997) was presented as a special episode to mark the 25th anniversary of Columbo. It was aired in 1997, 25 years after the first episode in Season One in 1971, and 29 years after the pilot Prescription: Murder in 1968.

**31**

Columbo is famous for his love of chilli con carne. This is a stew made up of meat chili peppers, garlic, tomato, onion and cumin. Pinto or kidney beans are added. Chili is Mexican or Texan in origin and there are many variations such as different meats, meat free, green chills and so forth.

**32**

The lake where negative reaction murderer Paul Galesko and Alvin Deschler meet inn Negative Reaction (1974) is the Hollywood Reservoir, Hollywood Hills, Los Angeles, California, USA.

**33**

The show has been described by the BBC as "timeless"

**34**

Theresa Goren's Malibu beach house in Murder in Malibu (1990) is the same house belonging to Joanna & Charles Clay in the Last Salute to the Commodore (1976) aired 15 years earlier.

The address is 33148 Pacific Coast Highway, Malibu, California, USA.

**35**

The episode Murder by the Book in 1971 was directed by Steven Spielberg. Spielberg never directed another episode and went on to be one of the most famous figures of all time in the film industry.

Spielberg said "I looked at every television episode I directed as a stepping stone to getting someone to hire me to direct a feature, So I used the television opportunities to try to do things that would make people think I could do feature films". He soon got the job of directing tv movie Duel because of the Columbo episode.

**36**

When the first season of Columbo was in production the original plan was for a new episode to air every week. An episode would have been shot every five days. Peter Falk did not want this as he made films and could not commit to this filming schedule for Columbo. Instead Columbo was shown once a month on a Wednesday.

**37**

In Agenda for Murder (1990) a piece of evidence implicating the murderer involves a bitemark on a piece of cheese. In 1999 doubts about forensic dentistry were raised. Since 2016 bite mark analysis has little support as evidence in legal cases.

**38**

The white house on the water in Dead Weigh (1971) that belongs to Maj. Gen. Hollister was, in real life, actually owned by Peter Falk, and is located in Newport Beach, California.

**39**

Peter Falk planned to make a final episode entitled Columbo's Last Case in the 2000's. But his failing health and lack of interest from tv networks meant it was not made.

**40**

Peter Falk added Columbo's cigar habit. In real life he was a cigarette smoker.

**41**

The quickest murder in the series is in Suitable for Framing (1971) occurring only about a minute into the episode.

**42**

The first episode filmed in the first series of Columbo was Death Lends a Hand (1971). It was the second episode aired in Season One.

**43**

For Season One, the producers Levinson and William Link carefully planned all the episodes. But as the show received great ratings Universal Studios asked for an extra episode for the season. Short Fuse (1972) became an extra episode and was filmed last. This episode was quickly put together and as a result many critics and fans believe it to the weakest in the first season of Columbo.

**44**

Murder by the Book (1971), the first episode of Season One of Columbo was ranked no 16 in a TV Guide poll of the 100 greatest tv episodes of all time conducted in 1997.

**45**

The theatre Frame and Stanhope perform Macbeth in in Dagger of the Mind (1972) is the Royal Court theatre in

London. Situated in Sloane Square it is a Grade II listed building. The building opened in 1888. It is the home of the English Stage Company known for its contemporary plays.

## 46

Columbo's clothes were Peter Falk's. He purchased the famous raincoat and the crumpled suit and shoes were his.

## 47

Even though Anne Francis's character is killed after 15 minutes in A Stitch in Time she has second billing behind villain Leonard Nimoy.

## 48

Columbo's famous battered old car is a Peugeot 403. The car was in production from 1955 to 1966. The model Columbo drives is a 1959 Peugeot 403 Cabriolet convertible.

## 49

In Uneasy Lies the Crown (1990) John Roarke plays himself in a poker game. Impressionist, actor and voiceactor Roarke does impressions of: John Wayne, Woody Allen, George Bush, Ronald Reagan, and Jack Nicholson.

## 50

In 2012 a poll for Best in TV: The Greatest TV Shows of Our Time Columbo was rated number 3 of all time legal or cop shows.

**51**

In An Exercise In Fatality (1974), Columbo said of Mrs Columbo's weight: "She was always a happy woman but for a while got depressed, thought she was getting too fat; she was binging on lasagna and rigatoni. But a TV exercise show saved our marriage"

**52**

In the The Most Crucial Game (1972) Valerie Harper has top guest star billing, but does not appear until three quarters of the way in the episode.

**53**

Peter Falk said that the ideas for the professions of murders came from looking through the yellow pages. One time the yellow pages opened up at Magicians. And thus the idea for the magician murderer The Great Santini in Now You See Him (1976) came about.

**54**

Columbo is a real Italian name, but the name was changed to Colombo when shown in Italy.

**55**

Short Fuse (1972) was Peter Falk's least favorite of the first season's episodes.

**56**

Columbo's famous car is often depicted as as unreliable and in need of repairs. In reality this annoyed Peugeot as it showed their cars in a bad light.

## 57

The showing a short clip teaser of the episode at the very start started from Season Two.

## 58

In Uneasy Lies the Crown (1990) Columbo asks for cream (milk) in his coffee when at the home of the murderer. He normally has his coffee black

## 59

The producers William Link and Richard Levinson said that the inverted mystery format where the murder is shown at the start of the episode posed difficulties when writing numerous other episodes.

"We had no idea that it would become an eventual trap for us and for all of the other writers who would bang their heads against the wall of the inviolate "Columbo" format."

## 60

In Murder Under Glass (1978) Columbo states that his father was born in Italy.

## 61

During the filming of Dead Weight (1971) there were tensions between Peter Falk and the producers and studio Universal. Falk felt that Universal were not fulfilling their promise of letting Falk direct some episodes of Columbo. He left the set stating he was ill. Universal threatened to sue and Falk had to return. During Falk's absence scenes had been shot using a stand in for Falk, and the crew refused to reshoot scenes with Falk.

## 62

In Death Hits The Jackpot (1991) it is apparent that Columbo is celebrating his 25th wedding anniversary. He mentions it in discussions with colleagues and he shops for a present.

## 63

Season Six of Columbo which ran from October 10 1976 to May 22 1977 only has three episodes: Fade in to Murder (1976), Old Fashioned Murder (1976) and The Bye-Bye Sky High IQ Murder Case (1977).

## 64

In The Conspirators (1978) none of the main four characters playing Irish people are from Ireland. Clive Revill (Joe Devlin) is from New Zealand. Jeanette Nolan (Kate O'Connell) is American. Bernard Behrens (GHeorge O'Connell) is from England. Michael Horton (Kerry Malone) is American.

## 65

In Now You See Him (1976) the scene where Columbo interviews a character called Lally played by Mike Lally in the boarding house was filmed months after the rest of the episode was filmed.

The plot twist featuring Lally as a witness who revealed Santini's identity had not been completed. Peter Falk wrote and directed the scene.

**66**

Robert Vaughn features in two Columbo episodes as Hayden Danziger in Troubled Waters (1975) and Charles Clay in Last Salute to the Commodore (1976).

Vaughn (1932 – 2016) had a distinguished career appearing in numerous television episodes as well as film and theatre. His most notable roles were as Napoleon Solo in the 1960s spy series The Man from U.N.C.L.E and as Gunman Lee in The Magnificent Seven (1960). Although a respected actor he was a cult actor especially in his appearances in comedy action tv shows. Vaughn received a Ph.D. in communications from the University of Southern California in 1970.

**67**

When Columbo arrives at a crime scene he either has coffee in a flask or asks for some.

**68**

Peter Falk bought the famous Columbo raincoat for $15 in 1967.

**69**

Columbo first aired in Italy in 1977 and the character was renamed Colombo.

The voice of Peter Falk was dubbed by Gian Piero Albertini. After the death of Albertini after the episode Murder, a Self-portrait the dubbing was taken over by Antonio Guidi.

**70**

In An Exercise in Fatality (1974) Milo Janus, played by Robert

Conrad, is 53 years old. Conrad was only aged 39 at the time.

**71**

Columbo Likes the Nightlife (2003) co stars Matthew Rhys and Peter Falk appeared together in the BBC Television adaptation of The Lost World in 2001. In The Lost World Peter Falk played an extremist religious character and murderer with Rhys as the hero.

**72**

In Playback (1975) Columbo stated has tried a portable tape dictaphone for his notes as he keeps losing his pencil. But he kept recording other dialogue by mistake - such as talking to his dog.

**73**

David Koenigauthor of 2021's book Shooting Columbo writes:

"The most important factor to Columbo's success was the casting of Peter Falk. Yet each episode's murderer often received as much—if not more—air time than the cop. So frequently casting just the right actor in the role could mean the difference between satisfactory and sensational [episode]. "

**74**

It's All in the Game (1993) is the second Columbo episode where the murderer tries to change Columbo's clothes. A tie is bought for Columbo which he wears in meetings with her.

In Requiem for a Falling Star (1973) the murderer also has a new tie bought for Columbo.

**75**

The interiors and stage for Now You See Him (1976) were filmed at The Magic Castle - 7000 Franklin Av Los Angelès, California, USA. The Magic Castle is located in Hollywood and a famous private club for magicians and fans of magic. It is the home of the Academy of Magical Arts. It was built in 1909 in a French chateau style and opened as The Magic Castle in 1963. The club is said to be haunted by the ghost of legendary escape artist Harry Houdini!

**76**

Peter Falk would improvise a lot of a scene and add ad libs. For example he would search for something in his coat pockets, or ask for a pencil. Columbo would talk about his wife and ramble on about random things to annoy the actor playing the suspect for the purposes of the scene.

**77**

Peter Falk rated Jack Cassidy highly as an actor. Cassidy appears in three episodes of Columbo turning in a wonderful performances as the villain: Murder by the Book (1971), Publish or Perish (1971) and Now You See Him (1976).

**78**

Troubled Waters (1975) stars Robert Vaughn and Patrick Macnee also appeared together in The Return of the Man from U.N.C.L.E. (1983).

**79**

In The Most Crucial Game (1972) Columbo says Mrs Columbo complains that the ice cream man comes before dinnertime and spoils "the child's" appetite.

**80**

For the casting of Playback (1975) Peter Falk travelled to Switzerland to ask Oskar Werner to play the villain.

**81**

In Columbo Goes to the Guillotine (1989) a framed poster of the Amazing Randi is on Max Dyson's workshop. The Amazing Randi is James Randi, a magician who debunked psychics and magicians, especially those who were making money from their fraudulent magic. The character of Max Dyson is based on Randi and Dyson is also a debunker of phony psychics.

**82**

The United States Copyright Office maintains a list of literary works which have been registered for copyright purposes with many writings which have never been published. There are numerous unused Columbo episodes on file.

Columbo:  News At Eleven

DATE REGISTERED: November 25, 1998

AUTHOR(s): Jones, Richard David, 1965-

Columbo : Now You See Him, Now You Don't

DATE REGISTERED: November 30, 1998

AUTHOR(s): DAngeli, Frank Paul, 1961-

Columbo :  Help Yourself

DATE REGISTERED: June 08, 1998

AUTHOR(s): Goubet, Stephane Olivier, 1972-

Columbo : Murder By Suicide

DATE REGISTERED: March 13, 1998

AUTHOR(s): DAngeli, Frank Paul, 1961-


Columbo's Big Surprise : A Comedy/Murder In Three Acts /
by Kitty Czarnelki

DATE REGISTERED: August 16, 1996

AUTHOR(s): Czarnecki, Kitty, 1959-


Columbo :  A Deadly Opportunity

DATE REGISTERED: November 16, 1995

AUTHOR(s): VanderLugt, Christopher, 1972-


Columbo : The Conscience Of The King

DATE REGISTERED: October 27, 1994

AUTHOR(s): Carriere, Carolyn J., 1955-


Columbo :  Don't Look A Gilt Horse In The Mouth

DATE REGISTERED: May 31, 1994

AUTHOR(s): Schleicher, Donna J., 1947-


Chemical Reaction : A Columbo  Movie Of The Week / written
by Catherine LaMoreaux and Lawrence Paone

DATE REGISTERED: March 11, 1991

AUTHOR(s): LaMoreaux, Catherine, 1959-; Paone, Lawrence, 1960-

Columbo  in The Greatest Night In The History Of Fights

DATE REGISTERED: April 09, 1991

AUTHOR(s): Leventon, Leonard

Columbo  : Take My Life, Please! / by Douglas Scott Williams

DATE REGISTERED: May 22, 1989

AUTHOR(s): Williams, Douglas Scott, 1972-

Columbo  : Color Number Game

DATE REGISTERED: November 09, 1983

DATE OF CREATION: 1972

AUTHOR(s): Downey, John Thomas, 1929-; Downey, Richard Thomas, 1960-; Downey, Robert Michael, 1962-

"Why Can't I Be Like Lieutenant Columbo ?"  [Musical work - Words and music by Tom Babcock]

DATE REGISTERED: August 31, 1979

DATE OF CREATION: 1979

AUTHOR(s): Babcock, Thomas Allan, 1954-

And finally, we find this intriguing entry in the records of the United States Patent and Trademark Office:

**83**

The construction site in Blueprint for Murder (1972) is of the Century City Plaza building and parking garage at 1801 Century Park E, Los Angeles, CA 90067.

**84**

Honor Blackman plays murderer Lillian Stanhope in Dagger of the Mind (1972). Blackman (1925-2020) was a highly respected English actress who appeared in numerous roles many utilising her glamorous persona. She had numerous film, tv and theatre roles. Her most famous was as one of the most memorable Bond girls Pussy Galore James Bond film Goldfinger (1964).

**85**

Dabney Coleman made two appearances on Columbo. In Double Shock (1973) he plays a detective - Detective Murray. In Columbo and the Murder of a Rock Star (1991) he plays the murderer, arrogant defense lawyer Hugh Creighton. Coleman (1932-) is a highly regarded character actor who has had many roles. He often plays slightly crooked, smarmy characters.

**86**

In Suitable for Framing (1971), Dale Kingston at one point removes several paintings from a wall. Tracy O'Connor then looks at the wall, admiring the paintings including some which Kingston had taken down!

**87**

Numerous actors were considered for each role in an episode of Columbo in the 1970s. The producer started the casting process. A list of actors for each part would be drawn up and scripts would be sent ot talent agencies for their ideas.  Finally the director, studio and television network Universal and NBC, and Peter Falk would be asked for their ideas.

## 88

In Columbo Goes to College (1990), Columbo is a guest lecturer in a criminology class. He discusses a recent episode's case - from Agenda to Murder (1990) - explaining how he matched teeth marks belonging to Oscar Finch (Patrick McGoohan) on a piece of cheese.

## 89

In the 1970s Columbo television network NBC submitted a wish list of guest stars for the show:

Bill Bixby
Richard Boone
Lloyd Bridges
James Caan
Glenn Corbett
Robert Culp
Tony Curtis
Sammy Davis Jr.
Glenn Ford
Jim Franciosa
Ben Gazzara
Michael Condon
Jerry Lewis
Jim Nabors
David Niven
Anthony Quinn
George Segal
William Shatner
McLean Stevenson
Robert Vaughan
James Whitmore
Efrem Zimbalist Jr.

Hersehel Bernardi

## 90

In Forgotten Lady (1975) The Wheeler Willis residence is at 141 N Grand Ave, Pasadena, California, USA.

## 91

No Time to Die (1992) is a unique Columbo episode as it does not feature a murder and Columbo never meets the main criminal.

## 92

Columbo uses the inverted mystery form where the murder is shown at the start of the story rather than the end. This was invented by English writer R. Austin Freemanearly in the 20th century.

Freeman asked himself:

"Would it be possible to write a detective story in which, from the outset, the reader was taken entirely into the author's confidence, was made an actual witness of the crime and furnished with every fact that could possibly be used in its detection?"

He wrote a book of short stories called The Singing Bone where the murderer is revealed at the start of the stories to test his idea. It was published in 1912.

## 93

In Murder Under Glass (1978) Columbo says Mrs Columbo is a "lousy cook"!

**94**

Columbo Cries Wolf (1990) is a unique episode as the victim is not killed in the first act. Also the planning and murder itself is not shown. Columbo solves a murder that was not a murder as the victim is shown to be alive! Of course the "victim" is then murdered for real and Columbo has to solve that murder.

.

**95**

John Finnegan (1926-2012) was an American character actor who appears in 12 episodes of Columbo in various roles. These include as policemen ans latterly as Barney owner of Columbo's favourite chill restaurant.

John Finnegan Columbo roles:

Blueprint for Murder (1972) – Carl
The Most Dangerous Match (1973) – Workman
Lovely But Lethal (1973) – Sergeant
A Friend in Deed (1974) – Lt. Duffy
Last Salute to the Commodore (1976) – Guard
Fade in to Murder (1976) – Assistant Director
Columbo Cries Wolf (1990) – Police Chief
Columbo and the Murder of a Rock Star (1991) – Chief Quentin Corbett
It's All in the Game (1993) – Barney
Strange Bedfellows (1995) – Barney
A Trace of Murder (1997) – Barney
Columbo Likes the Nightlife (2003) – Sean Jarvis

**96**

Roddy McDowall's character in Short Fuse (1972) Roger Stanford is an amateur photographer who has his own darkroom on the office premises. In real life, McDowall was a keen photographer famous for the photos he took of film and tv stars.

## 97

In Columbo Cries Wolf (1990) Columbo is investigating the murder of a woman from Los Angeles who did not arrive at a meeting in London. Columbo says he is investigating the murder for his friend Detective Chief Superintendent Durk of Scotland Yard who appeared in Dagger of the Mind (1972).

## 98

At the end of Last Salute to the Commodore (1976) Columbo is rowing off in a boat and Sgt. Kramer asks him about smoking:

Kramer: "Thought you were gonna quit;" Columbo: "Not yet. No, not yet, Sergeant. Not yet".

This is reference to speculation that it was going to be the last Columbo episode.

## 99

Bing Crosby was considered for the role of Columbo. Iconic singer and actor Crosby was born in 1903 and died in 1977 when the seventies Columbo was still running. He turned down the role as he thought it would take too long to film and he wanted to enjoy his later years and his hobby golf.

## 100

The number plate of Columbo's car in the seventies series was 044-APD. When the series returned in 1988, the number plate was 448-DBZ.

**101**

Kim Cattrall appears as Joanne Nicholls in How to Dial a Murder (1978).

Cattrall was born in Liverpool, England in 1956. Columbo was an early role for Cattrall who went on to appear in many films and tv shows as well as highly regarded theatre work. Her most iconic role was as Samantha Jones in tv series Sex and the City (1998–2004).

**102**

Fisher Stevens is the youngest actor to be arrested by Columbo. He was 25 years 3 months old when Columbo Goes to the Guillotine (1989) was first shown.

**103**

Some of the main cast of monkey themed science fiction film Planet of the Apes (1968) appear in Columbo - not wearing monkey make up! Kim Hunter plays Zira in Planet of the Apes. In Columbo she plays Edna Matthews in Suitable for Framing (1971)

Roddy McDowall plays Cornelius in Planet of the Apes. He plays Roger Stanford in Short fuse (1972)

Maurice Evans plays Dr Zaius in Planet of the Apes. He appears in Forgotten Lady (1975) as Redmond the Butler.

**104**

By Dawn's Early Light (1974) is the only episode of the four Patrick McGoohan appeared in that he did not direct.

**105**

The funeral home in A Friend in Deed (1974) in the stock footage is not actually in California. It is the Ephrussi de Rothschild villa and gardens in Saint-Jean-Cap-Ferrat on the French Riviera. This location also appeared in the James Bond film Never Say Never Again (1983).

**106**

Peter Falk chose his iconic Columbo car from a selection of old cars on the NBC studio lot. The car did not have an engine.

**107**

In The Greenhouse Jungle (1972) Columbo walks down a steep grassy hill to inspect the wreckage of the Jaguar car. He stumbles and falls down the hill falling on his back. This actually happened: Peter Falk fell and it was kept in the scene.

**108**

In Double Shock (1973) Columbo has a memorable scene where he joins Dexter Paris on his cooking tv show. This scene was improvised by Peter Falk and Martin Landau (Dexter Paris).

**109**

The title of Dagger of the Mind (1972) comes from the famous soliloquy in William Shakespeare's "Macbeth" (Act II, Scene I, lines 33-39):

"Is this a dagger which I see before me, / The handle toward my hand? Come, let me clutch thee: / I have thee not, and yet I see thee still! / Art thou not, fatal vision, sensible / To feeling as to sight? Or art thou but / A dagger of the mind, a false creation, / Proceeding from the heat-oppressed brain?"

## 110

When the series was brought back in 1988 new Columbo television network ABC used three Peugeot 403 convertibles cars for Columbo's car.

## 111

The aerial tramway in Short Fuse (1972) is The Palm Springs Aerial Tramway in Palm Springs, California. Square tram cars were used at the time - now round ones are used.

## 112

In Identity Crisis (1975) Columbo says Mrs Columbo enjoys classical music especially Ludwig van Beethoven and Wolfgang Amadeus Mozart. Her favorite piece is Giacomo Puccini's "Madame Butterfly".

## 113

Death Lends a Hand (1971) saw the first appearance of iconic Columbo villain Robert Culp in Columbo.

## 114

Fred Draper (1922-99) appears in six episodes of Columbo in small roles. He is unique in that he had only a small role as Swanny Swanson in Last Salute to the Commodore (1976) but was the murderer.

His Columbo roles were:

Lady in Waiting (1971) – Cab driver (uncredited)

Lovely But Lethal (1973) – Dr Murcheson
Negative Reaction (1974) – Crime lab guy (uncredited)
A Deadly State of Mind (1975) – David Morris
Last Salute to the Commodore (1976) – Swanny Swanson
Fade in to Murder (1976) – Joseph

## 115

In A Case of Immunity (1975) Jeff Goldblum is an extra in the crowd demonstrating in the scene outside of the legation. This was one of Goldblum's first roles and he went on to become a huge film star with roles in films such as Jurassic Park (1993) and Independence Day (1996).

## 116

In Columbo Goes to the Guillotine (1989) Columbo states he's never seen anything like the guillotine trick. But in Now You See Him (1976) He goes to a magic shop where the shopkeeper shows him a guillotine trick using a carrot and then Columbo's hand.

## 117

In Étude in Black (1972) The Maestro's house exterior is the same one used in television series The Fresh Prince of Bel-Air (1990).

## 118

American character actor Stephen Elliott (1918-2015) appears in two Columbo episodes: A Deadly State of Mind (1975) where he plays Carl Donner (the murder victim) and Grand Deceptions (1989) where he plays General Padget. In both episodes his wife his having an affair with the murderer.

**119**

Columbo Goes to College (1990) is one of the few Columbo episodes where Columbo appears before the murder happens.

**120**

The $300,000 ransom in The Greenhouse Jungle (1972) is worth nearly $2.1 million at 2023 prices.

**121**

It's All in the Game (1993) is the only episode - apart from the two pilot episodes - where Peter Falk as Columbo appears onscreen a the starting credits; normally Peter Falk and Columbo are shown separately.

**122**

In Now You See Him (1976) Columbo has a change of image. He does not wear his raincoat - he has a new one he dislikes and says "he has had a hair cut",

**123**

A Bird in the Hand...(1992) is the only episode in which Columbo himself is a witness to a murder he solves.

**124**

In RIP, Mrs Columbo (1990) Columbo claims he and his wife never had any children even though he mentions them in other episodes. Maybe he lied to protect his family as he was talking to a murderer!

**125**

The campus scenes in By Dawn's Early Light (1974) were filmed at the Citadel in Charleston, South Carolina. It is a military college. One of six senior military colleges in the United States, it opened in 1842.

**126**

The yacht in Last Salute to the Commodore (1976) is an 85 foot super-yacht named the Mojo. It was built in 1969. Celebrities used it for parties and other functions - for example Barry White's ashes were scattered from it in a ceremony attended by Michael Jackson. George C. Scott and his wife Columbo actress Trish Van Devere chartered the yacht in 1978 when it was damaged in a storm. The boat was lengthened to 100 feet during expensive repairs, and the boat remains in service for events and cruises today in Newport Beach, California.

**127**

George Gaynes(1917-2016) has two roles in Columbo. Étude in Black (1972) as Everett and Any Old Port in a Storm (1973) where he played a Frenchman - a wine expert who helps Columbo. both were bit parts. Gaynes most famous role was as Commandant Eric Lassard in the Police Academy 80s comedy film series.

**128**

The helicopter (N32PM) used to spread the ashes in Ashes to Ashes (1998) is a 1994 Eurocopter AS350 B2 Ecureuil Squirrel/AStar.

**129**

In Uneasy Lies the Crown (1990) Columbo says he had been in

the force 22 years. The first Columbo pilot Prescription: Murder was shown in 1968 ,22 years earlier.

## 130

The opening kaleidoscope-like images of Las Vegas in A Bird in the Hand...(1992) were used twenty years earlier to open the Banacek episode A Million the Hard Way.

## 131

The last ever episode of Columbo was Columbo Likes the Nightlife broadcast on January 30, 2003.

## 132

The character of Columbo first appeared in a 1960 episode of the anthology series The Chevy Mystery Show. The episode was entitled Enough Rope. This was adapted by Richard Levinson and William Link from their short story May I Come In. The story is about a police lieutenant then named Fisher. Bert Freed (1919-94) played Columbo. Freed was a prolific character actor on film and tv.

## 133

The pawnbrokers in Strange Bedfellows (1995) where Graham McVeigh buys a gun is located at Sunset Pawnbrokers - 1647 N La Brea Ave, Los Angeles, California, USA.

## 134

Columbo Cries Wolf (1990) is the first instance where a pop music song is played: She Drives Me Crazy by Fine Young Cannibals.

**135**

The football game footage in A Bird in the Hand...(1992) is from a Canadian Football League in Edmonton between Saskatchewan Roughriders and the Edmonton Eskimos

**136**

The reason Columbo drove a  dilapidated car down car that was always breaking down is the writers thought it would match Columbo's appearance and personality.

**137**

The Columbo episode Requiem For A Falling Star (1973) starring Johnny Cash was originally titled Murder by Starlight.

**138**

In 1988 co creator of Columbo William Link thought that it was time to bring Columbo back - it had been off air since 1978. He successfully pitched the idea of a new Mystery Movie series including Columbo to television network ABC.

**139**

Patrick McGoohan was asked if he would play Columbo in 1977 if a new actor was needed. McGoohan said no as in his opinion only Peter Falk could play Columbo.

140

For Negative Reaction (1974) producer Everett Chambers complied a list of 25 names to play the villain Paul Galesko. These included Alan Arkin, Orson Welles, Martin Balsam,

John Cassavetes, Joel Gray, Tony Randall, James Mason, Donald Pleasance, Hal Holbrook, Patrick McGoohan, Tony Franciosa, Richard Benjamin, Louis Jordan, Robert Duvall, Arthur Hill and Peter Sellers.

The role went to Dick Van Dyke.

## 141

Horror legend and iconic actor Vincent Price, who appears in Lovely but Lethal (1973) said that Columbo is "really simple and also redoubtable and complex."

## 142

The artist who created the portrait of Columbo in Murder, a Self Portrait (1989) is Jaroslav Gebr. Gebr (1926-2013) was born in Czechoslovakia. He fled communist Czechoslovakia and moved to the US and worked in film and television art departments of MGM, Fox and Universal Studios. He created pictures, visual effects and other art used in the production of film and television. Gebr painted pictures for specific use in film and tv productions. He also created album covers and portraits of actors. Another distinctive piece of work of Gebr was the portraits in Rod Serling's anthology horror tv show The Night Gallery.

## 143

In Mind Over Mayhem (1974) mentions his children, stating that his "wife and kids are visiting the mother-in-law."

## 144

In Prescription: Murder (1968) Columbo states Mrs Columbo wants him to get psychiatric help as he "bothers people".

**145**

When the first Columbo series came to an end in 1978 Universal sold the 1959 Peugeot 403 Cabriolet he drove. When the series returned in 1989 Peter Falk thought the car was still in Universal Studios's parking lot. The car was located in Ohio.

**146**

In The Greenhouse Jungle (1972) plays pool with Jarvis Goodland at Goodland's house. The position of the balls changes from when we first see the ball table to when Columbo takes his first shot.

**147**

Eddie Albert plays the murderer in Dead Weight (1971). He did not get on with Peter Falk on set. Albert said to Falk: "I always wanted to meet you, I always wanted to work with you, but you're a real asshole."

**148**

In Any Old Port In A Storm (1973) Columbo says says he went on a picnic with the wife and kids, and later in the same episode and "my kid". He might have had another child too young for the picnic, because in the same episode he says he "needs a babysitter and buys 2 quarts of milk: you know how it is when you have kids."

**149**

Columbo Likes the Nightlife (2003) was the 69th and final Columbo episode. As with the finale of many TV series, there was nothing special about the episode that celebrated a long running series coming to the end.

## 150

William Shatner said of his character Fielding's Chase's mustache in Butterfly in Shades of Grey (1994):

"I went back to review some of the footage and I have to tell you, I lost track of the dialogue so quickly because I became simply riveted by the terrible, pencil-thin prosthetic mustache they put me in. Go back and look at the episode and tell me you're not distracted by that thing! Not only was it a poor mustache, but in half the scenes it sags to the left or the right. How the makeup folks—and I, for that matter—could have allowed that to happen, I will never know. The episode is fun, and it was a treat working with Peter again, but that mustache… that mustache…"

## 151

In Short Fuse (1972) The blue Mercedes convertible driven by Patrick O'Neal is the same one (license number XSM 494) driven by Jack Cassidy in Murder by the Book (1971). The killer uses the car to transport the victim in the trunk in both episodes.

## 152

Columbo often buys his hot dogs from Arthur who runs a hot dog stand at Travel Town, which is a real place in Griffith Park, Los Angeles.

## 153

Columbo got small speaking parts for his friends Dick Lance and Mike Lally in Columbo Negative Reaction (1974).

**154**

In Murder, a Self Portrait (1989) Max Barsini is possibly called Barsini as he paints a bar scene in the episode.

**155**

In Ashes to Ashes (1998) the exterior for the mortuary was Laury's Restaurant Garden Center and Retail Shop located in Glendale. The area had been closed for a year and contained a big car part which was perfect for the scenes of the helicopter taking off and landing and related scenes involving the helicopter.

**156**

Columbo Goes to the Guillotine (1989) was the last directorial credit of Sam Wanamaker.

**157**

When creating Columbo, William Link and Richard Levison wanted to create a slightly fantastical world rather than a gritty realistic view of Los Angeles crime: "

"We would create a mythical Los Angeles and populate it with affluent men and women living in the stately homes of the British mystery novel."

**158**

Murder by the Book (1971) is the first episode in which Columbo's Peugeot 403 car appears.

**159**

In Lady in Waiting (1971) when offered cream for his coffee, Columbo turns it down, saying he has his coffee black; but he already is seen drinking a white coffee.

**160**

In Identity Crisis (1975) director Patrick McGoohan inserted many references to his cult television series, The Prisoner (1967) including his The Prisoner catchphrase "Be seeing you!" and on one occasion in Columbo wearing an outfit similar to that which had been his outfit in The Prisoner.

**161**

A Stitch In Crime (1973) was originally titled The Specialist

**162**

By the Dawn's Early Light (1974) featured father and son Bruce Kirby and Bruno Kirby In the credits they were listed as Bruce Kirby Sr and B Kirby Jr.

**163**

William described Peter Falk as being "a joy to work with" on Fade in to Murder (1976)

"I felt honored to be asked to be on Columbo. It was a prestigious show in the public consciousness and the Nielsen ratings, but more importantly, it was considered a New York actor's show. It was filmed in the days when you could be a working actor there: there were plenty of film, television and theater opportunities in New York".

**164**

No Time to Die (1992) is one of the few episode where Columbo appears at the start.

**165**

Columbo creators William Link and Richard Levison said this about the tone of Columbo:

"We made other decisions those first weeks, the most basic of which was that the series would not be what is known as a "cop show." We had no intention of dealing with the realities of actual police procedures. Instead, we wanted to pay our respects to the classic mystery fiction of our youth, the works of the Carrs, the Queens, and the Christies. We knew that no police officer on earth would be permitted to dress as shabbily as Columbo, or drive a car as desperately in need of burial, but in the interest of flavorful characterization, we deliberately chose not to be realistic.

Our show would be a fantasy, and as such it would avoid the harsher aspects of a true policeman's life: the drug busts, the street murders, the prostitutes, and the back-alley shootouts."

**166**

The last episode of Columbo - Columbo Likes the Nightlife (2003) was broadcast in 2003 as part of ABC Thursday Night at the Movies.

**167**

In Double Exposure (1973) the plot relies on effectiveness of subliminal cuts in films and Kepple mentions that the Consumer Trade Commission had banned such cuts. But the use of such subliminal advertising has never been proved to be particularly effective, and no such ban was made.

**168**

Columbo's first name was the basis of a legal dispute between a trivia expert and the makers of iconic board game Trivial Pursuit.

Trivia encyclopedia author Fred L. Worth placed a number of false facts in his books. If they appeared elsewhere then he knew that the fact had been copied and could sue for copyright infringement. One of his false facts was that Columbo's first name was Philip. In 1984 a version of Trivial Pursuit was released with this fact as one of the questions. Worth files a lawsuit demanding $300 million from Trivial Pursuit.

Jusdges denied Wortg's claim for compensation. Trivial Pursuit admitted thet used encyclopedias such as Worth's for questions; and Columbo's first name is not Philip!

**169**

Peter Falk was the first actor to be nominated for an Oscar and Emmy in the same year - receiving supporting actor nomination for Murder Inc and an Emmy for supporting actor in television program The Law and Mr. Jones.
He was the first actor nominated for an Oscar and Emmy the same year.

**170**

From 1976 Peter Falk said he would like to play Columbo forever but with one or two appearances a year so he could make films too,

**171**

Playback (1975) is the only episode in which Columbo fires a gun.

**172**

Last Salute to the Commodore(1976) saw the second appearance in Columbo of Wilfrid Hyde-White. He plays Kittering, Esq. In Dagger of the Mind (1972) he plays Tanner, butler of Sir Roger Haversham.

Wilfrid Hyde-White. (1903-1991) was an English character actor. Charming typically English Hyde-White had numerous roles on films, television and the stage ans lived in the US later in his life.

**173**

When William Shatner played television detective Ward Fowler in Fade in To Murder (1976) there were a number of in jokes with Fowler's egotistical behaviour on set and arguments with the crew mirroring Peter Falks's disputes with the makers of Columbo.

**174**

In Budapest, Hungary there is a life sized bronze statue of Columbo. Situalted on Falk Miksa Street, it depicts Columbo looking confused wearing a raincoat and holding a cigar.

It is thought that the actor is a relative of the street's namesake, a 19th-century Hungarian political figure. It was placed there in 2014 costing of $63,000.

**175**

Columbo ran for 35 years and a total of 69 episodes between 1968's Prescription: Murder and 2003's Columbo Likes the Nightlife.

**176**

In Murder, a Self Portrait (1989) Max Barsini's painting of Vito's Bar is similar in composition, colours and theme to Edward Hopper's Nighthawks Style.

**177**

In Undercover (1994) the art gallery owner refereed to Mo Wineburg as 'something out of a Rocky movie'. Mo Wineburg was played by Burt Young who plays Paulie, Rocky's brother and law and friend in the Rocky movies.

**178**

In Columbo Likes the Nightlife (2003), Columbo doesn't make an appearance until 00:30 minutes into the show.

**179**

Peter Falk appeared as Columbo in a 3 minute Alias sketch produced for a 2003 TV special celebrating the 50th anniversary of ABC. Alias is a science fiction/thriller series which ran from 2001-2006.

**180**

Ashes to Ashes (1998) was the final television and final on-screen performance for Patrick McGoohan.

**181**

In Dead Weight (1971) detective fiction books by Mrs. Melville from Murder by the Book (1971) are seen on General Hollister's bookshelf.

**182**

Ross Martin, who plays the killer in Suitable for Framing (1971), was Peter Falk's camp counselor; Falk was 12 and Martin was 19. Later Martin taught Falk acting.

**183**

The original title for Short Fuse (1972) was Formula For Murder.

**184**

Peter Sellers was offered the part of murderer Paul Galesko in Negative Reaction (1974) but wanted $360,000 to play the part. Dick Van Dyke played the role.

**185**

There are four murders that take place outside US territory.

Matter of Honor (1976) takes place in Mexico. Dagger of the Mind (1972) takes place in Britain. Troubled Waters (1975) takes place on a cruise ship in international waters. A Case of Immunity (1975) takes place in a foreign embassy in Los Angeles which has extraterritorial status.

**186**

When Columbo first meets Nelson Brenner in Identity Crisis (1975) in the hallway outside the lecture room, Columbo hands a photo to M Brenner who gives it back to Columbo. In the next shot Brenner has the photo and as he walks away hands it to Columbo again.

**187**

A Bird in the Hand...(1992) is the final Columbo episode written by veteran Columbo writer Jackson Gillis. His first screenplay was for Suitable for Framing (1971).

**188**

A Columbo episode normally has the same structure. The first scene contains the murder. In the second scene the police discover the murder. Columbo appears about 20 minutes into the episode wanting to look at the body. He is normally concerned with procuring coffee, finding somewhere to the eggshells from his boiled egg or finding a pencil. Next Columbo's tries to catch the murderer looking for a small mistake the murderer has made to incriminate his/her self.

**189**

Although Columbo often talks about his relatives, No Time to Die (1992) is the only episode to feature any of them: his nephew Detective Andy Parma.

**190**

Katey Sagal hasd an early role in Columbo in the episode Candidate for Crime (1973). The episode was directed by her father Boris Sagal. Boris also directed another Columbo The Greenhouse Jungle in 1982. Sadly Boris died in a helicopter accident while directing tv mini series World War III in 1982.

Katey is know for playing Peggy Bundy in sitcomMarried... with Children (1987–1997), Leela on animated comedy Futurama (1999–2003, 2008–2013, 2023) and Gemma Teller Morrow in biker crime drama Sons of Anarchy (2008–2014).

**191**

In Mind Over Mayhem (1974) the computer room sets are reused from science fiction film The Andromeda Strain (1971).

**192**

Columbo hides his genius for crime deduction and solving by adopting a friendly, bumbling charming persona.

**193**

In The Bye Bye Sky High IQ Murder Case 1977 Columbo says Mrs Columbo is "a whiz" at crossword puzzles.

**194**

The show went on hiatus after The Conspirators in May 1978. Columbo was never cancelled and negotiations to return continued. There was always a will to keep Columbo alive and make more episodes.

**195**

The music playing in the club in Columbo Likes the Nightlife (2003) is by The Crystal Method, specifically two songs from their Tweekend album Roll it Up and Wild, Sweet and Cool.

**196**

In Forgotten Lady (1975) Columbo says he likes to go bowling and it therapeutic: "When I'm down in the dumps, I go bowling."

**197**

William Shatner said about Columbo:

"The key to the show's success was Peter Falk, who was a terrifically nice guy and a joy to work with. He knew that character inside out—not just what worked, but why it worked. The writers may have joked about paying Peter such an exorbitant salary but he was worth every penny, and the studio knew it."

**198**

Columbo's favourite chili restaurant Barney's Beanery is a real place. It is located Santa Monica Boulevard in West Hollywood. The restaurant has three rooms and seats 175 people and includes a bar and pool room. Opened in 1920s, Barney's Beanery has 40 types of chilli and other traditional fast foods.

Located on Santa Monica Boulevard in West Hollywood, the legendary Barney's Beanery is a three-room, roadhouse style bar/restaurant/pool-room that has been a Hollywood staple since the 1920s patronised by numerous celebrities. Barney's is a true haven for hard-core chili buffs, offering 40 different recipes of chili, plus 140 kinds of hamburgers, dozens of beers on tap and hundreds more brands in bottles.

**199**

Stephen J. Cannell also submitted an on spec script during the 1973 Writers Guild of America screenwriters strike. This was filmed as Double Exposure (1973), a classic Columbo with Robert Culp.

Cannell (1941-2010) wrote and created numerous tv series even though he had dyslexia. His most famous creation was the The A-Team (1983–1987).

**200**

In Columbo Goes To College (1990) Columbo says he is taking medication to lower his cholesterol.

**201**

In The Bye-Bye Sky High I.Q. Murder Case (1977) Jamie Lee Curtis has a brief speaking part as a waitress who takes umbrage at Columbo bringing a doughnut into a restaurant. This was one of Curtis's early roles and she was 18 at the time. she has had many roles since, her most famous as Laurie Stode in the Halloween film series.

**202**

Marcia Wallace is not credited in Lady in Waiting (1971), even though she had a speaking part during the inquest scene. There may have been a mix-up during production of the first season as she is credited in Murder by the Book (1971) even though she doesn't appear in it.

**203**

The young Italian waiter in Mario Murder Under Glass (1978), is played by Antony Alda. He is the real-life brother of Alan Alda who among numerous other roles played Hawkeye Pierce in M*A*S*H. Sadly Antony died in 2009 aged 52.

**204**

Columbo was parodied in Mad magazine as Clodumbo. It was published in the January, 1973 issue and a satire of Columbo's pestering. The suspect is Dr Robert Culpable.

## 205

Patrick McGoohan won an Emmy (Outstanding Single Performance by a Supporting Actor in a Comedy or Drama Series - 1975) for his performance as Colonel Lyle C. Rumford in By Dawn's Early Light (1974).

## 206

Now You See Him (1976) was originally titled Quicker Than the Eye in a first draft dated January 29, 1975.

## 207

Faye Dunaway won a Primetime Emmy Award for Outstanding Guest Actress in a Drama Series for It's All in the Game (1993).

## 208

A Matter Of Honor (1976) was originally titled A Matter of Bravery.

## 209

Columbo pilot Ransom for a Dead Man (1971) was released theatrically in the UK.

## 210

Dead Weight (1971) and A Stitch in Crime (1973) both had scenes filmed at the Los Angeles Petting Zoo.

**211**

Nine actors played the murder victim in one episode and a non victim in another episode.

These are:

Leslie Nielsen is the murder victim in Identity Crisis (1975) and non-victim in Lady in Waiting (1972).

Tim O'Connor who is the victim in an Old Fashioned Murder (1976) and non-victim in Double Shock (1973).

Anne Francis who is the victim in a A Stitch in Crime (1973) and non-victim in Short Fuse (1972).

Ida Lupino who is the murder victim in Swan Song (1974) and a non-victim in Short Fuse (1972).

John Dehner who plays the victim in Last Salute to the Commodore (1976) and non-victim in Swan Song (1974).

Sorrell Booke who plays the victim in the The Bye-Bye Sky High I.Q. Murder Case (1977) and non-victim in Swan Song (1974).

Dean Stockwell who is the victim in The Most Crucial Game (1972) and a suspect in Troubled Waters (1975).

Stephan Elliott is the victim in A Deadly State of Mind (1975) and non-victim in Grand Deceptions (1989).

James Gregory is the victim in Short Fuse (1972) and non-victim in The Most Crucial Game (1972).

**212**

Vito Scotti starred in six episodes of Columbo:

Any Old Port in a Storm (1973) – Maitre d'

Candidate for Crime (1973) – Chadwick
Swan Song (1974) – Mr. Grindell
Negative Reaction (1974) – Thomas Dolan
Identity Crisis (1975) – Salvatore Defonte
Murder, a Self Portrait (1989) – Vito

Scotti (1918-1996) was an American character actor known as a man of a thousand faces for his ability to play different roles. He had numerous roles in tv, film and on Broadway.


## 213

A decision was made by the creators to keep the series non violent. The murders are sanitised. Columbo does not (apart from on a few rare occasions) carry a gun, have a fight or a car chase.


## 214

Joyce Jillson played Joan, the fiancee of the victim in Any Old Port In A Storm (1973).

Jillson (1945-2004) had a few tv and film roles before finding greater fame as an astrologer. Called the Astrologer To The Stars she even became personal astrologer to President Ronald Reagan in the 1980s. She was astrologer for 20th Century Fox Studios in the 70s suggesting astrologically favourable dates for film openings. Her astrology column was syndicated in 200 publications worldwide.


## 215

Columbo Goes to College (1990) is the first episode where Columbo is one of the first to discover the victim (with a group of students he has been lecturing to).

**216**

In Murder Can Be Hazardous To Your Health (1991) Columbo gives his view on computers: he says "these machines baffle me!"

**217**

Timothy Carey appears in two episodes of Columbo: Dead Weight (1971) and Fade In To Murder (1976). In both episodes he runs a restaurant and helps Columbo with his opinions on the cases. Carey (1929-1994) had numerous film and tv roles and specialised in violent characters.

**218**

William Shatner on Columbo:

"Columbo was a difficult show to write for, since the audience already knew who the killer was within the first twenty minutes and before the erstwhile detective appeared on the scene. The challenge was to keep the audience entertained as they watched Columbo figure out what they already knew. This challenge is one of the reasons they only produced as many episodes as the writers and Peter felt they could do well. Season six featured only three, for instance."

**219**

The first episode of Columbo was the first pilot Prescription: Murder broadcast on February 20, 1968.

**220**

Throughout An Exercise in Fatality (1974) hints are given to Columbo's solving of the crime. Columbo ties his shows on numerous occasions, there is a lingering close up of the victim's shows, and Columbo discusses his shows with other people. There is a character names Lacy in the episode.

## 221

Columbo's creators wanted the show would be the American equivalent of the English drawing room murder mystery, "dependent almost entirely on dialogue and ingenuity to keep it afloat."

## 222

Peter Falk had these observations about the episode Forgotten Lady (1975):

"Peter spoke of what a pleasure it was for him to work with Janet Leigh. He also enjoyed the humorous interplay between Columbo and the snobby butler, Maurice Evans.

Falk enthusiastically praised the writers, saying that "they really outdid themselves", that Columbo's observations were very good here, and that this episode was "one of our better efforts".

He said that the "first investigation scene," where Columbo picks up a series of small clues that the death was not a suicide, was later used as a model, to show other "Columbo" writers how these scenes are supposed to be done.

And he described this episode as "a real rarity" because of the unusual ending where Columbo does not bring in the murderer."

## 223

Columbo Goes to the Guillotine (1989) was the first episode of Columbo for a decade. Peter Falk was 61 years old when the episode was made.

**224**

Jonathan Demme directed one episode of Columbo: Murder Under Glass in 1978. Demme (1944-2017). Demme directed The Silence of the Lambs in 1991 and won an Oscar for Best Director. He was a noted director of music concert films.


**225**

Peter Falk's 2006 autobiography was titled Just One More Thing after Columbo's catchphrase.


**226**

In Death Lends a Hand (1971) Brimmer offers Columbo a $30,000 a salary to work for his security firm. That would equate to around $200,000 at 2023 prices.


**227**

Murder, a Self Portrait (1989) is one of the few episodes where Columbo is seen before the murderer or the murder..


**228**

In Last Salute To The Commodore (1976) Columbo says Mrs Columbo wants him to quit smoking cigars because she says "the smoke is harmful to her plants."


**229**

In Candidate For Crime (1973) Columbo says that Mrs Columbo "belongs to a bowling league -- they have an annual dinner dance, $17.50 per couple."

**230**

The exterior location for Matilda's Art Gallery in Suitable for Framing (1971) is at 653 N. La Cienega Boulevard, West Hollywood, California, USA

**231**

In Étude in Black (1972) it is revealed Columbo's salary as a police detective is $11,000. This is about $76,000 in 2023.

**232**

In Dead Weight (1971) General Hollister has duplicate books on his bookshelf. There are two of the same Mrs Melville mystery; three copies of Challenge - one upside down, two copies of High Season and several other multiple copies if the same book.

**233**

In Publish or Perish (1974), when Columbo opens up Eddie Kane's address book to look at Greenleaf's number, the closeup is the same one as the earlier shot when Greenleaf did the same thing and includes Greenleaf's latex gloved finger!

**234**

In No Time To Die (1992) Columbo says his wife "loves to dance."

**235**

In 1979 negotiations for the NBC next series of Columbo stalled because Peter Falk wanted no time or budgetary constraints on the Columbo episodes.

**236**

Bruce Kirby roles in nine episodes of Columbo.

Lovely But Lethal (1973) – Lab attendant
By Dawn's Early Light (1974) – Sergeant George Kramer
A Deadly State of Mind (1975) – Sergeant George Kramer
Identity Crisis (1975) – Sergeant George Kramer
Last Salute to the Commodore (1976) – Sergeant George Kramer
Make Me a Perfect Murder (1978) – TV repairman
Columbo Cries Wolf (1990) – Sergeant George Kramer
Agenda for Murder (1990) – Sergeant George Kramer
Strange Bedfellows (1995) – Sergeant Phil Brindle

Kirby played Sergeant Kramer in six episodes and Kramer was the most recurring character apart from Columbo and Columbo's dog.

Bruce Kirby (1925-2021) had numerous roles on film and particularly on tv utilising his character actor skills.

**237**

The Columbo production team considered up to thirty different actors for every role in every episode.

**238**

In Death Lends a Hand (1971) the murderer Brimmer says that 10% of the world's population is ambidextrous - left handed. In reality only 1% of people are left handed.

**239**

In the British set Dagger of the Mind (1972) the scenes involving British actor Wilfrid Hyde-White were filmed in California. He owed money to British tax authorities and could not go to Britain.

## 240

Columbo cannot stand the sight of blood. In Forgotten Lady (1975) he says: "Just the sight of blood makes me sick."

## 241

In Mind Over Mayhem (1974) a strange guest star is a robot who provides an alibi for the murderer.

The robot prop was first used as Robby the Robot in the 1956 science fiction film Forbidden Planet. The robot cost $125,00 to create - about $1 million in 2023 prices. The robot appeared in many tv shows and films: Robby had the nickname of "the hardest working robot in Hollywood.". In 2017 Robby was sold for S$5,375,000 at an auction by Bonhams Auctioneers in New York making Robby the most expensive film prop ever sold at auction.

## 242

In Short Fuse (1972) zany murderer Roger sprays Silly String over Columbo and others. Silly String was not patented until December 1972 and Short Fuse aired in January 1972. The prop person on the episode presumably got hold of a prototype can.

## 243

William Shatner on his character Ward Fowler in Fade in to Murder (1976):

"Peter Falk had made the show enormously popular and had been rewarded with many industry awards and ever-fatter pay checks to keep coming back for additional seasons. The writers created the guest character of highly paid TV procedural actor Ward Fowler (whom I portrayed); Fowler himself played the titular character on the popular TV series Detective Lucerne. In-jokes abounded, such as the studio arguing about the obscene amounts of money Fowler was demanding to renew his contract. 'Ward Fowler is not the first actor on this network to win an Emmy,' one of them remarks, an all-too-obvious poke at Peter Falk, who had won back-to-back Emmys for the two previous seasons of the show.

I felt honored to be asked to be on Columbo. It was a prestigious show in the public consciousness."

## 244

Catherine McGoohan, Patrick McGoohan's daughter, plays the funeral home assistant in "Ashes to Ashes (1998). McGoohan plays the funeral home owner. Catherine McGoohan (1952-) has appeared in numerous television and film roles such as Elizaberthtown (2005).

## 245

In Murder Under Glass (1978) Columbo reveals Mrs Columbo attends night school and is studying for her "final exam in accounting."

## 246

Richard Levinson and William Link won an Emmy for Outstanding Writing for Death Lends a Hand (1971)

## 247

In Mind Over Mayhem (1974), Columbo describes his wife's important role in his crime-solving methods:

"When a case gets too tough, I gotta talk to my wife. She doesn't talk about the case, she talks about everything else." In other words, she helps him to think. Her interests are so broad and so varied, that she is always likely to say something to trigger a crucial inspiration."

## 248

Columbo's family is intriguing and mysterious as he incessantly talks about his wife, but she is never seen. Also he discusses his other family - cousins, nephews, children etc - but they are never seen and the viewer is unsure whether Columbo is inventing family members for the purposes of his interactions with the murderer.

## 249

Writer Steven Bochco had this to say on the character of murderers in Columbo:

"The murderer is always very rich and arrogant. That's why the passage when Columbo try to catch him was so pleasant for the televiewers."

## 250

The Stanford Chemical Plant scenes in Short Fuse (1972) were filmed at Union Carbide in Torrance, CA.

## 251

Columbo enjoys hard boiled eggs, especially when attending crime scenes. He has a habit of leaving shells at the crime scene annoying the forensic investigators so one of his first jobs is to find somewhere to put the egg shell"

**252**

Fourteen-year-old Caroline Treynor in In The Bye-Bye Sky High I.Q. Murder Case (1977), 14 year old Caroline Treynor is played by 21-year-old Carol Jones.

**253**

Columbo says his wife is a voracious reader of newspaper. In The Conspirators (1978) he says: "she reads the whole newspaper, including the obituaries, the personals, and even the shipping news...".

**254**

The Paradise Cove location where Louise's body is recovered in Murder, a Self Portrait (1989) is the same location used for Jim Rockford's house trailer in The Rockford Files (1974).

**255**

Like Dead Weight from earlier in the season, Lady in Waiting (1971) from season one of Columbo saw arguments between Peter Falk and the production team.

Executives at Universal suggested that for future seasons Peter Falk would play Columbo for one episode with other actors playing Columbo in other episodes!

**256**

Peter Falk was an accomplished charcoal drawing artist. In the 90s he created a portrait of his most famous character - Columbo. In 2000 it was sold on Ebay in March 2000 for $1000.

**257**

Ken Franklin and Ferris's office in Murder by the Book (1971) is located at 9000 West Sunset Blvd., West Hollywood, California, USA.

**258**

In Identity Crisis (1975) Brenner states his music in his home is hydroponic. But this is a water based agriculture system. The writers presumably meant quadraphonic (4 channel 4 speaker super-stereo).

**259**

In the opening scene of Troubled Waters (1975) Columbo describes his wife when asking if anyone has seen her on the cruise ship. She is shorter than Columbo and has long black hair worn in a bun.

**260**

Peter Falk at one stage insisted he would not appear in Dead Weight (1971) stating that he was sick. The studio threatened to sue Falk who then returned to the set.

**261**

A producer had this to say on battles with Peter Falk in the first season of Columbo:

"...we were all involved in intrigues worthy of John le Carre. Falk insisted that someone he trusted be placed on our staff to look out for his interests. As soon as this was done, we noticed that he somehow mysteriously managed to acquire advance copies of our scripts in outline and rough first drafts. These were not nearly ready to be seen; quite naturally, he was dissatisfied with them and tended to view with suspicion our promises that they would be improved by rewriting. We countered his ploy by keeping all material under lock and key. He made it a habit to drop by the editing rooms to monitor the progress of various segments. We instructed our editors to close their doors or to actually leave the building if Falk approached. When he insisted on watching dailies, we wrote scenes that had to be filmed away from the studio, scheduling them so that he would be on location when dailies were shown."

## 262

In Mind Over Mayhem (1974) Columbo makes reference to his "wife and kids".

## 263

In Forgotten Lady (1975) Columbo reveals he bowls with his wife, who belongs to a league, and sometimes he goes bowling with his friend Harry.

## 264

In Rest In Peace, Mrs Columbo (1990) Columbo says his wife has "never had her picture taken - she believes she looks lousy in photographs".

## 265

Orson Welles was considered for the part of The Great Santini in Now You See Him? (1976) but he asked for too much money.

**266**

Dennis Dugan had a part in (1976) as Sergeant Mac Albinsky who assists Columbo. Dugan (1946-) is also a director and has directed many films and television episodes. He directed a Columbo - Butterfly in Shades of Grey (1994).

**267**

Dead Weight (1971) is the first of three episodes where the murderer is a military man. The other two are By Dawn's Early Light (1974) and Grand Deceptions (1989).

**268**

In A Stitch in Crime (1973), Columbo breaks the shell on his boiled egg breakfast on the murder weapon!

**269**

In The Conspirators (1978), Columbo says he would like to have a pinball machine in the living room but his "wife would never go for it."

**270**

Ed Begley Jr. (1949-) appears in two Columbo episodes: How To Dial a Murder (1978) as Officer Stein and Undercover (1994) as Irving Krutch.

Begley was friends with Peter Falk in real life.

**271**

When Columbo returned in 1989 after a decade long hiatus, The Orlando Sentinel wrote:

"How great is it to have Columbo back?"

The South Florida Sun Sentinel stated:

"The return of Columbo is like a reunion with a very special friend, someone with whom your bond is so warm and affectionate that even after a decade, there is no awkward feeling of estrangement."

## 272

Columbo does not like guns. The only time he fires a gun in the series is when he test fires one into a box of sand in Playback (1975); when a gun needs to be test fired into a mattress in Troubled Waters (1975) he gets another person to do it.

## 273

Carlene Watkins is listed the end credits of "The Bye-Bye Sky High I.Q. Murder Case" as playing Amy but doesn't appear onscreen.

## 274

Columbo suffers from aviophobia - fear of flying. In Ransom for a Dead Man (1971) the murder Leslie Williams tries to get Columbo to leave her alone by making Columbo ride with her in a small plane.

## 275

Columbo says that he takes his coffee "hot, strong and black - none of that de-caf stuff!". He often arrives at a crime scene with a plaid thermos flask of coffee.

**276**

Columbo likes three sugars in his tea and hates it lukewarm.
In Butterfly in Shades of Grey (1994) he has honey in his tea to
try and stave off a cold.

**277**

Rosanna Huffman plays Tracy O'Connor in Suitable for
Framing (1971) and Mrs Thornwood in Rest in Peace, Mrs.
Columbo (1990). Huffman (1938-2016) was married to
Columbo creator Richard Levinson.

**278**

Peter Falk said Any Old Port in a Storm (1973) is his personal
favorite episode. He praised the "skills and performance" of
Donald Pleasance who plays the murderer.

**279**

The house where Oscar Finch kills Frank Staplin in Agenda
for Murder (1990) is located at 400 North Amapola Lane, Bel
Air, Los Angeles, California, USA.

**280**

In the series Columbo drinks cream soda stating he is "a cream
soda kinda guy"; hot chocolate; malt drink; root beer;
bourbon; ginger ale; iced tea; seltzer; scotch; beer; sherry; and
red wine.

**281**

Peter Falk chose Columbo's shoes; they were actually his own
shoes. He found the old high topped shoes in his closet and

thought they suited Columbo as they looked "looked like something an Italian immigrant would wear."

## 282

How To Dial A Murder (1978) had two alternative titles: The Laurel and Hardy WC Fields Citizen Kane Murder Case and "Snips And Snails And Murderer's Tails!

## 283

Columbo is from a Catholic Italian-American background. Actor Peter Falk is of Jewish Russian and Polish descent.

## 284

Two episodes of Columbo, No Time to Die (1992) and Undercover (1994), were based on the 87th Precinct novels by Ed McBain did not strictly follow the standard Columbo/inverted detective story format.

Ed McBain is a pseudonym of Evan Hunter. 55 87th Precinct novels were written between 1956 and 2005. No Time to Die (1992) was based on So Long as You Both Shall Live 1976). Undercover (1994) was based in Jigsaw (1970). A friend had suggested to Peter Falk that the Ed McBain books would make good stories for Columbo episodes, so Falk bought the rights to two of the stories to adapt.

## 285

Peter Falk praised Patrick McGoohan for his work on Identity Crisis (1975). McGoohan wrote his own character's dialogue.

Falk stated:

"In this episode, the scenes between Columbo and the

murderer are, in my judgment, among the best we ever did. They have that perfect balance between being both compelling and amusing. And that's what we always strive for -- that's the trick in those scenes, keep them tense and keep them funny. And a great deal of credit for that goes to Patrick.

McGoohan....I'll always remember how much fun I had playing them, and to this day I get a kick out of watching them."

## 286

The actor playing the author murder victim Alan Mallory in Publish or Perish (1974) is Mickey Spillane. Crime novelist Spillane created the iconic Mike Hammer detective character. There have been many Hammer novels, short stories and film and television adaptions.

## 287

Peter Falk himself directed the last episode of the first season Blueprint for Murder (1972).

## 288

Last Salute to the Commodore (1976) is a traditional whodunit episode where the murderer is not known until the end. It even includes a classic whodunit element where all the suspects are gathered in a room and murderer is revealed.

## 289

Mrs Columbo is not a fan of Columbo's suit! In Columbo Goes To College (1990) says "she's gonna send Columbo's suit out to be cleaned and burned."

**290**

In Murder, A Self-Portrait (1989) Max Barsini creates a portrait of Columbo.

Barsini begins by warning Columbo that he might not like what the portrait reveals:

"Barsini: "Your policeman's soul!...Dark, tormented, pitiless!...The policeman unmasked!...You may be shocked!

Columbo: "It's very nice, Sir. I think you've been teasing me...Do you think I could show that to Mrs Columbo?"

**291**

A Columbo culinary specialty is a peanut butter and raisin sandwich. He makes this in Murder of a Rock Star (1991) and It's All in the Game (1993).

**292**

Columbo normally whistles the tune This Old Man as the pieces in his murder mystery case begin to fall into place.

**293**

In A Stitch In Crime (1973) Columbo says he gets "queasy around illness" or hospitals and that he "actually faints".

**294**

Caution: Murder Can Be Hazardous To Your Health (1991) was originally titled Smokescreen.

**295**

In Any Old Port in a Storm (1973) Ric Carsini's age is said to be "29 on his next birthday." Gary Conway, the actor playing Ric, was actually 37 years old at the time of filming (born February 4, 1936).

**296**

Peter Falk wrote the episode entitled It's All in the Game (1993).

**297**

Columbo has a fear of heights - acrophobia. In Swan Song (1974) he evrn says "I don't even like being this tall."!

**298**

Although Columbo is on "the ship" with his wife in Troubled Waters (1975) she is never actually seen by the viewer. Some of the ship's crew do mention seeing her.

**299**

Columbo has said he eats chili every day of his life. For variety he chili with beans, and chili without beans, on alternate days "for "variety."

**300**

In Murder Under Glass (1978) Columbo shows his culinary skills by preparing a dish of veal scaloppini for murderer Paul Gerard in Vittorio's kitchen.

**301**

Shera Danese was Peter Falk's second wife; they married in 1977. She appears in 6 episodes of Columbo: Fade in to Murder (1976), Murder Under Glass (1978), Murder, a Self Portrait (1989), Columbo and the Murder of a Rock Star (1991), Undercover (1994) and A Trace of Murder (1997). She was the murderer in A Trace of Murder.

**302**

In Murder Under Glass (1978) murderer Paul Gerard refers to Mary Choy's restaurant as The House of Choy when discussing her name appearing in Vittorio's date-book. Later, Columbo meets with bankers over coffee cake, and Mary Choy's restaurant is called The House of Shanghai,"

**303**

Bing Crosby was asked to play Columbo in the first pilot, but pulled out because shooting was scheduled opposite a golf tournament he was playing in.

**304**

In Strange Bedfellows (1995) Columbo discussed a Mrs Columbo cure for a bad stomach. When Columbo got food poisoning from bad clams she treated him with soup made from chicken-fat and lentils.

**305**

In Murder Under Glass (1978) Columbo discussed his wife's cookery skills: "she is a remarkable woman...has lots of interests, but cooking isn't one of them."

**306**

Patrick McGoohan holds the record for appearances as the murderer with four roles. Robert Culp and Jack Cassidy played the murderer three times.

**307**

Columbo is not a fan of elevators. He says that elevators are "another one of my problems" in Troubled Waters (1975), and that "elevators make his ears pop" in Swan Song (1974).

**308**

The jazz club set in Etude In Black (1972) was used for the basement of the wax museum in Dagger of The Mind (1972).

**309**

Ken Franklin's lake house in Murder by the Book (1971) is located at 933 Deer Trail Lane, Big Bear Lake, Big Bear Valley, San Bernardino National Forest, California, USA.

**310**

There were no Christmas/Holiday set episodes of Columbo. But a Christmas Columbo novel was written in 1972. A Christmas Killing was written by Alfred Lawrence. In the novel Columbo investigates the murder of a young apartment store window dresser.

**311**

In Death Lends A Hand (1971) it is said Mrs Columbo "says Columbo doesn't have enough ambition."

**312**

Although Short Fuse (1972) was the last episode of the first season of the series to be filmed, it aired before Blueprint for Murder (1972).

**313**

In Grand Deceptions (1989) starts to wear glasses on occasion to read. By Death Hits The Jackpot (1991) he has fixed his broken glasses with a paperclip!

**314**

Columbo hates guns so much that he evades the mandatory Los Angeles Police Department marksmanship test for ten straight years. When threaten with suspension if he does not take the test he pays a sergeant 5 dollars to take the test for him!

**315**

Lisa Chambers's apartment in Double Shock (1973) is located at 4455 Los Feliz Blvd., Los Angeles, California, USA.

**316**

Oliver Brandt's residence in The Bye-Bye Sky High I.Q. Murder Case (1977) is located at 10451 Bellagio Road, Los Angeles, California, USA. It has since been demolished.

**317**

In An Exercise in Fatality (1974) Columbo and Milo Janus run along the beach near Paradise Cove - 28128 Pacific Coast Highway, Malibu, California, USA.

**318**

Arlene Martel appears in three episodes of Columbo: as Gloria The Greenhouse Jungle (1972), as Tanya Baker in Double Exposure (1973) and as salesgirl in A Friend in Deed (1974). Martel (1936-2014) had many character roles on film and television. Her skill at creating different characters and accents earnt her the nickname The Chameleon. A notable role was as Spock's bride in the Star Trek episode Amok Time (1967).

**319**

Famous director Brian De Palma co wrote a script with Jay Cocks. for Columbo and submitted it in July 1973. Entitled Shooting Script, the plot revolved around a crime documentary maker who films a murder he carried out on video camera.

**320**

Short Fuse (1972) was originally titled Formula for Murder.

**321**

Columbo enjoys his chili with some ketchup, salt and crushed saltine crackers. In Ransom for a Dead Man (1971) he says: "You see, it's the crackers that make the dish."

**322**

A Columbo Detective Game was released by Milton Bradley in 1973. In this Cluedo style game, Players compete to be the first to either solve the mystery (collect four cards to create one figure, four cards to create one weapon, and one Motive card) or find Columbo (collect all six Columbo cards plus the one "It's a Mystery to Me" card).

Peter Falk did not allow his likeness to be used so in the box art Columbo is looking away and we see the back of his head.

## 323

In Ransom for a Dead Man (1971) Margaret is watching the film Double Indemnity (1944) when arguing with Lesilie in the kitchen. In Double Indemnity a woman kills her husband to claim an insurance payout.

## 324

The flight in the mountain range in Ransom for a Dead Man (1971) is in the Tehapachi Mountains, California, USA.

## 325

In Grand Deceptions (1989),when Columbo looks at the body of Sergeant Major Lester Keegan, Keegan can be seen to be blinking.

## 326

In Mind Over Mayhem (1974) it is revealed that Mrs Columbo's mother lives in Fresno, California.

## 327

By Dawn's Early Light (1974) is the only time in the original series where someone asks what Columbo's first name is. Patrick McGoohan's Colonel Rumford  asks, and Columbo replies: "I do have a first name, but my wife is about the only one who uses it."

**328**

Uneasy Lies The Crown (1990) used an old script that had been rejected for a Columbo. Steven Bochco originally wrote this script in 1973 for the third season, but it was not made because Peter Falk felt the villain was not interesting enough. It was used for the 1977 McMillan & Wife episode Affair of the Heart. McMillan & Wife was a detective series starring Rock Hudson. It ran from 1971 to 1977 and was part of the NBC Mystery Movie Series with Columbo.

It was decided to use the script for the Uneasy Lies The Crown Episode. One of the poker plays in the Columbo episode Nancy Walker was a cast member of McMillan and Wife, and Columbo jokes that she was on that "the Rock Hudson mystery show".

**329**

Perhaps the strangest casting is Horror icon Vincent Price appears in Lovely But Lethal (1973), but not as the murderer. Instead he plays the president of a women's cosmetics company.

**330**

In Columbo Cries Wolf (1990), The postcard that Diane sends from Milan has an English postage stamp on it!

**331**

Columbo first orders chili in Barney's Beanery in Ransom for a Dead Man (1971).

**332**

In Agenda for Murder (1990) murderer Oscar Finch is leading

defense lawyer practicing in Los Angeles for 20 years; but he has never heard of Columbo or his cases!

## 333

In Dagger of the Mind (1972) Nicholas and Lilian play Macbeth at the Royal Court Theatre, Sloane Square, Belgravia, London, England, UK.

## 334

The indoor cemetery and crematorium scenes in Ashes to Ashes (1998) were filmed at Universal Studios, Hollywood, Los Angeles, California, USA.

## 335

In Murder, A Self Portrait (1989) it is revealed that Mrs Columbo is fascinated dreams and often writes them down.

## 336

A long writers strike by the Writers Guild of America from March to August, 1988 delayed the return of Columbo in the late 80s and limited the season to four episodes when Columbo returned in February 1989.

## 337

In Rest In Peace, Mrs Columbo (1990) Columbo says Mrs Columbo says her husband has "a closed mind about movies, books and music."

**338**

Dr. Eric Mason's residence in How to Dial a Murder (1978) is located at 2411 Glendower Ave, Los Angeles, California, USA.

**339**

In Any Old Port in a Storm (1973) Adrian Carsini feared that his beautiful winery would be purchased and ruined. In real life, the Mirassou Winery, where filming of the episode took place, was bought by Gallo in and demolished. A housing development occupies the land now. Gallo bought the rights to the Mirassou brand.

**340**

In Rest In Peace, Mrs Columbo (1990) Columbo says that Mrs Columbo thinks "chili is going to kill him."

**341**

For the part of murderer Paul Galesko in Negative Reaction (1974) Alec Guinness was considered. He did not play the part which went to Dick Van Dyke, but he appear with Peter Falk in comedy detective spoof Murder by Death in 1976.

**342**

In Swan Song (1974) Columbo eats some chili at the murderers party. He enjoys until being told that it was made with squirrel meat.

**343**

An Exercise In Fatality (1974) Columbo says that although Mrs Columbo "struggles with her weight" he never "wouldn't let her be too thin."

## 344

A Friend in Deed (1974) was released in the cinema in some European nations.

## 345

Étude in Black (1972) is the episode which saw the debut of Dog, Columbo's pet basset hound.

## 346

Marcia Wallace is listed as Woman in Murder by the Book (1971). But Wallace does not appear in the episode. She does appear in another episode in the first season Lady In Waiting (1971) as a woman at the inquest who predicts Beth will go free saying : "Jupiter and Venus are in good aspect with Pluto." She is not credited for this episode. The mix is is obviously a production mistake where her credit is on the wrong episode. Wallace later voiced Mrs Krabappel on The Simpsons.

## 347

Peter Falk on Columbo's raincoat:

"In 1966, for example, I was walking on the 57th avenue in New York when it started to rain. I entered a shop and I bought a raincoat. When I had to find one for Columbo, I simply took this one. Columbo wore that raincoat until 1982. Then, the costumier made another one on the same pattern."

**348**

For the part of murderer Paul Galesko in Negative Reaction (1974) Peter Ustinov was considered. He did not play the part which went to Dick Van Dyke.

**349**

Billy Goldenberg's soundtrack to Ransom for a Dead Man (1971) was released.

**350**

The top is down on Columbo's famous Peugeot Covertable in Short Fuse (1972), Lady in Waiting (1971), The Most Dangerous Match (1973), Last Salute to the Commodore (1976) and Columbo and the Murder of a Rock Star (1991).

**351**

Character actor Mike Lally appeared in 25 episodes of Columbo. This makes him the actor to appear in thr most episodes of Columbo apart from Peter Falk. Most of his roles were as bartenders investigators etc with little dialogue.

**352**

The Conspirators (1978) was written as a pilot for another series and adapted for a Columbo episode.

**353**

In Columbo Goes to College (1990) The tips of the main rotor blades of the filming helicopter can be seen at the top of the screen during the opening sequence depicting aerial shots of California.

**354**

Perino's Restaurant in Murder Under Glass (1978) is located at 4101 Wilshire Boulevard, Los Angeles, California, USA. The building was demolished in 2005 and an apartment block was built on site.

**355**

The Carsini Winery in Any Old Port in a Storm (1973) was located at 2880 E Airport Dr, Ontario, California, USA.

**356**

In Troubled Waters (1975) Columbo reveals his wife "likes to have a good time, and sometimes she gets carried away."

**357**

Vincent McEveety (1929-2018) directed seven episodes of Columbo between 1990-1997: Rest In Peace, Mrs Columbo (1990), Death Hits the Jackpot (1991), A Bird in the Hand ... (1992), It's All in the Game (1993), Undercover (1994), Strange Bedfellows (1995), and A Trace of Murder (1997). He directed numerous television episodes of popular series. Also directed an umber of Disney films during the 1970s.

**358**

Jeffrey Reiner directed the last ever episode Columbo Likes the Nightlife (2003). Reiner (1960-)has directed and produced numerous television series.

**359**

The sea front house in Dead Weight (1971) is at located at 2

Collins Island, Collins Island, Balboa Island, Newport Beach, California, USA.

## 360

The university in Columbo Goes to College (1990) is Pepperdine University - 24255 Pacific Coast Highway, Malibu, California, USA.

## 361

The scenes where Lauren Staton purchases a tie for Columbo in It's All in the Game (1993) were filmed at Westfield Mall 6600 Topanga Canyon Blvd, Canoga Park, California, USA.

## 362

Bernard L. Kowalski (1929-2007) directed four episodes of Columbo between (1971-1976): Death Lends A Hand (1971), An Excercise in Fatality (1974), Playback (1975) and Fade in to Murder (1976). Kowalski has been described as "an important figure in television with a long and impressive list of credits."

## 363

When in A Friend in Deed (1974) Columbo is being paged over his car's police radio, for the only time in the series, his call number is revealed as "194".

## 364

The store where Ken Franklin makes his alibi call to Joanna Ferris, Jim's wife in Murder by the Book (1971) is at Juniper Point, 41365 N Shore, Big Bear, California, USA.

**365**

Season Ten of Columbo is not a traditional season of television, but a collection of 14 TV specials which aired between 1990 and 2003.

**366**

A total of 69 episodes of Columbo were produced, beginning with two pilot episodes which aired in 1969 and 1971.

**367**

The beach house in A Deadly State of Mind (1975) is located at 605 Paseo Del Mar, Palos Verdes Estates, California, USA.

**368**

Columbo Co-creator William Link had this to say about Jack Cassidy:

"Our favourite. He was juicy without going over the top. Jack had a wonderfully humorous utter contempt for this bug who wouldn't leave him alone: Columbo".

**369**

Peter S. Fischer (1938) wrote 7 episodes of Columbo: Publish or Perish (1974), An Exercise in Fatality (1974), A Friend in Deed (1974), Negative Reaction (1974), A Deadly State of Mind (1975), Rest in Peace, Mrs. Columbo (1993), Butterfly in Shades of Grey (1994).

He created popular tv detective show Murder, She Wrote with Columbo creators Richard Levinson and William Link.

**370**

Try and Catch Me (1977) was the first episode where Columbo was not shown as part of a Mystery Movie series with other shows such as Quincy and McMillan & Wife.

**371**

In Dagger of the Mind (1972) Columbo takes photographs of Tower Bridge, London, England.

**372**

Billy Connolly plays the murderer Findlay Crawford in the episode Murder With Too Many Notes (2000). Billy Connolly (1942-) is a popular Scottish comedian, actor, writer, television presenter and musician.

**373**

In Blueprint for Murder (1972) the location for Elliot Markham's office exterior was at Friars Club - 9900 S Santa Monica Blvd., Beverly Hills, California, USA.

**374**

Patrick McGoohan as has a strong link with Columbo appearing as the murder in four episodes:

Colonel Lyle C. Rumford  By Dawn's Early Light (1974), Nelson Brenner Identity Crisis (1975), (and directed), Oscar Finch Agenda for Murder (1990) (and directed), Eric Prince Ashes to Ashes (1998), (and directed).

He also directed Last Salute to the Commodore (1976) and Murder with Too Many Notes (2000).

McGoohan (1928 – 2009) was an Irish American actor, writer and director. He had many roles and his most famous were in spy television series  Danger Man (1960–1968) and The Prisoner (1967–1968).

## 375

Jackie Cooper (1922-2011) stars as the murderer Nelson Hayward in Candidate for Crime (1973).

Copper started as a child actor - nominated for an Oscar aged 11 for Skippy (1931). He had a distinguished career as an actor and director. One popular role was as newspaper editor Perry White in the Christopher Reeve Superman films between 1978-1987.

## 376

Tyne Daly appears in two episodes of Columbo: as Dolores McCain in A Bird in the Hand (1992) and as Dorothea McNally  in Undercover (1994). Daly is a distinguished film, television and theatre actress. A famous role of Daly's was in tv detective show Cagney & Lacey (1981–1988).

## 377

Héctor Elizondo appears as as Hassan Salah in A Case of Immunity (1975). Elizondo (1936-) is of Puerto Rican and Basque descent. A prolific actor on stage and screen, he is also a musician and dancer.

## 378

Ruth Gordon stars as murderer Abigail Mitchell  in Try and Catch Me (1977). Gordon (1896-85) was a distinctive actress through her long career. She was also a prolific writer.

**379**

Lee Grant stars as the murderer Leslie Williams in Ransom for a Dead Man (1971). Grant (1925-) has has a long career and has directed well regarded documentaries.

**380**

James Gregory stars in two episodes of Columbo as murder victim David Buckner in Short Fuse (1972) and as Coach Rizzo The Most Crucial Game (1972). Gregory (1911-2002) was a character actor specialising in brusque tough characters.

**381**

In Identity Crisis (1975) Columbo says Mrs Columbo is "crazy about music...Beethoven, that guy who wrote Marriage of Figaro...rock music too, it's on all the time when the nieces are over."

**382**

Columbo originally aired on NBC from 1971 to 1978 as one of the rotating programs of The NBC Mystery Movie series. Columbo then aired less ABC from 1989 to 2003 with occasional episodes.

**383**

In Lady In Waiting (1971) Columbo questions a suspect in a hair salon which has a deep pile carpet. Such as carpet would not pass heath and hygiene inspections.

**384**

Columbo uses circumstantial speech in his conversations with murder victims either naturally or on purpose to confuse the murder. Circumstantial speech includes rambling and unnecessary unrelated details to the conversation.


## 385

Laurence Harvey as murderer Emmett Clayton in The Most Dangerous Match (1973). Harvey (1928-1973) was born in Lithuania, moved to South Africa when young and then to England in 1945. Debonair and distinguished Harvey appeared widely on film, theatre and stage in Britain and the US.


## 386

The Conspirators (1978) was originally planned to air Feb 1978, and Make Me a Perfect Murder (1978) was going to be shown in May 1978.


## 387

Murder victim Gerry Winters's  house in Butterfly in Shades of Grey (1994) is located at 550 Latimer Rd, Santa Monica, California, USA.


## 388

William Shatner had this to say in his appearance in Butterfly in Shades of Grey (1994):

"In 1994, the new version of Columbo was in full swing. I had just a few years ago finished up the last of the six Star Trek films starring the original cast, and I was trying to be more selective with my roles. It was one of the rare times in my career in which I felt secure enough to do that, and sadly, it's a feeling that rarely lasts long. To my surprise and delight, I was invited to return to Columbo, which absolutely fit the bill of the kind of work I wanted to do. Last time, I had played a somewhat sympathetic actor, this time I was anything but sympathetic as the villainous talk-back radio host Fielding Chase."

**389**

Season One of Columbo consists of seven episodes.

**390**

In The Bye-Bye Sky High I.Q. Murder Case (1977) Theodore Bikel, who plays the murderer, appears as a member of the high Sigma Society peoples'- a Mensa-like society. He was was a real-life member of Mensa.

**391**

In A Friend in Deed (1974) John Finnegan plays Lt. Duffy and is called by that name several times. But the end credits list him as Lt. Dreyer.

**392**

Verity Chandler's house in Ashes to Ashes (1998) is located at 13439 Chandler Blvd, Sherman Oaks, Los Angeles, California, USA

**393**

No Time to Die (1992) is an adaptation on the Ed McBain 87th Precinct novel So Long as You Both Shall Live. Columbo is a composite of various police characters in the novel. In the novel Bert Kling's wife is kidnapped on their wedding day. In the Columbo episode Columbo's nephew's wife is kidnapped. with Columbo,

**394**

An Old Fashioned Murder (1976) was originally titled In Deadly Hate.

**395**

For the role of Negative Reaction (1974) Peter Falk wanted Peter Sellers to play murderer Paul Galesko. But Sellers wanted $360,000—18 times the most the show had ever paid for a guest star. Dick Van Dyke palyed the role.

**396**

A Deadly State of Mind(1971) is one of the few episodes of Columbo in which the original murder is a spontaneous act rather than meticulously planned.

**397**

Season Two of Columbo consists of eight episodes.

**398**

The last episode of the original seventies run of Columbo was The Conspirators broadcast on May 13, 1978

**399**

In A Bird In The Hand (1992) says of Mrs Columbo's crossword habit: "When she does crossword puzzles, she gets me to do them . It drives me crazy." - A

**400**

The rave warehouse in Columbo Likes the Nightlife (2003) is located at 590 South Santa Fe Avenue, Los Angeles, California, USA.

**401**

In Troubled Waters (1975) the filming location was a ship called The Sun Princess. Later sold numerous times it was named Ocean Dream when it sank off the coast of Thailand in 2016 near Laem Chebang Port and remains there.

**402**

Season Three of Columbo consists of eight episodes.

**403**

In Make Me A Perfect Murder (1978) Columbo says that Mrs Columbo "has been treated by an osteopath, who in turn referred me to a chiropractor."

**404**

The Conspirators (1978) was filmed at Los Angeles Harbor, San Pedro, Los Angeles, California, USA.

**405**

The horse ranch in Strange Bedfellows (1995) is located at Ventura Farms - 235 W. Potrero Road, Thousand Oaks, California, USA.

**406**

In Candidate for Crime (1973) when Nelson walks out on his balcony to fire the gun through the glass, the background view of the city behind him is actually a rather obvious painting with folds and brush marks.

**407**

James Frawley (1936-2019) directed six episodes of Columbo:

Try and Catch Me (1977), Make Me a Perfect Murder (1978), How to Dial a Murder (1978), Murder, Smoke and Shadows (1989), Sex and the Married Detective (1989) and Murder: A Self Portrait (1989).

An actor in the 60s. And 70s as well as a director, one notable directing job was The Muppet Movie (1979).

**408**

In Sex and the Married Detective (19890 Columbo gives his rather infamous tuba playing demonstration at theDorothy Chandler Pavilion, Los Angeles County Music Center - 135 N. Grand Avenue, Downtown, Los Angeles, California, USA.

**409**

Robert Donner(1931-2006) appears in three episodes of Columbo: as The Drunk in Any Old Port in a Storm (1973), Arnie in Caution: Murder Can Be Hazardous To Your Health (1991) and Zeke Rivers in Undercover (1994).

Donner had many roles in tv and film mostly playing oddballs. A notable role was as prophet Exidor in comedy show Mork and Mindy (1978-82).

**410**

The hospital exterior for A Stitch in Crime (1973) is the Sheraton Universal Hotel - 333 Universal Hollywood Drive, Universal City, California, USA.

**411**

Troubled Waters (1975) is one of the very few episodes of Columbo in which he appears on screen before the murder takes place.

**412**

For a homicide detective, Columbo is rather squeamish. Sometimes he cannot bear to look at a dead body or if he does only takes a quick peek.

**413**

Steven Spielberg said of his meeting with Columbo creators Richard Levinson and William Link:

"They wanted their show to look like a feature film.

That was my first experience with episodic television where the producers were encouraging me to make shots, whereas other television producers would beg me not to."

**414**

Season Four of Columbo has six episodes.

**415**

In Playback (1975) Columbo muses on Mrs Columbo's

painting skills: "she paints a little, a lot of landscapes, the kind where you paint by the number. They come out pretty good."

## 416

Dr. Wesley Corman's house in Uneasy Lies the Crown (1990) is located at 3535 Sweetwater Mesa Rd, Malibu, California, USA.

## 417

Dexter Paris's house in Double Shock (1973) is located at The Enchanted Hill - 1441 North Angelo Drive, Beverly Hills, California, USA.

## 418

The pier in A Stitch in Crime (1973) where Marcia & Dr. Mayfield go to meet, walk and talk is the Malibu Pier, Malibu, California, USA.

## 419

In Death Lends a Hand (1971), Arthur Kennicut's mansion is located at Beverly House - 1011 N. Beverly Drive, Beverly Hills, California, USA.

## 420

Ben Gazzara directed two episodes of Columbo: A Friend in Deed (1974) and Troubled Waters (1975).

Gazzara (1930-2012) was only an occasional director of tv shows and more known for his highly distinguished acting on film, tv and in the theatre. Gazzara met Peter Falk on the set of Husbands (1970) and the duo and actor/John Cassavetes director became close friends afterwards.

## 421

The exterior to the funeral home in Ashes to Ashes (1998) is 570 West Avenue 26, Los Angeles, California, USA

## 422

At aged 80 Ruth Gordon, who played Abigail Mitchell in Catch Me If You Can (1977), was the oldest actor to play a murderer in Columbo.

## 423

Lovely But Lethal (1973) was originally titled Beauty Is As Beauty Dies.

## 424

Seven actors played the murderer in one episode and a non murderer in another episode.

Robert Culp plays a non murderer in Columbo Goes to College (1990) and the murderer in Death Lends a Hand (1971), The Most Crucial Game (1972) and Double Exposure (1973)

Ray Milland plays a non murderer in Death Lends a Hand (1971) and the murderer in The Greenhouse Jungle (1972).

Patrick O'Neal plays a non murderer in Make Me a Perfect Murder (1978) and the murderer in Blueprint for Murder (1972).

Robert Vaughn plays a non murderer in Last Salute to the Commodore (1976) and the murderer in Troubled Waters

(1975)

Dabney Colman plays a non murderer in Double Shock (1973) and the murderer in Columbo and the Murder of a Rock Star (1991)

Joyce Van Patten plays a non murderer in Negative Reaction (1974) and a murderer in Old Fashioned Murder (1976).

Tyne Daly plays a non murderer in  Undercover (1994) and the murderer in A Bird in the Hand... (1992).

**425**

Season Five consists of six episodes.

**426**

Columbo Likes the Nightlife (2003) was the first widescreen Columbo to be in the widescreen format:  1.78 : 1.

**427**

Clifford Calvert's house in A Trace of Murder (1997) is located at 5148 Louise Ave, Encino, Los Angeles, California, USA.

**428**

The auditorium for Dr Mason's lecture and office in How to Dial a Murder (1978) is located at Harmony Gold Theater - 7655 Sunset Blvd, Los Angeles, California, USA.

**429**

Jack Smight (1925-2003) directed one episode of Columbo: Dead Weight in (1971). Smight directed a number of television episodes and feature films such as Midway (1976).

**430**

Columbo was intended to be cultured, stylish and smooth talking played by an actor such as Bing Crosby. Peter Falk introduced Columbo's ramblings, strange mannerisms and disheveled appearance.

**431**

Alan J. Levi (1960-) directed three episodes of Columbo Uneasy Lies The Crown (1990), Columbo and the Murder of a Rock Star (1991) and No Time to Die (1992).

**432**

In Ransom for a Dead Man (1971) Columbo has chili and talks to Margaret at Barney's Beanery - 8447 Santa Monica Blvd., West Hollywood, California, USA

**433**

The exterior building used as the London Wax Museum was in Dagger of the Mind (1972) was the Royal College of Music, South Kensington, London.

**434**

Fred Astaire was considered to play the murderer Paul Galesko in Negative Reaction (1974).

**435**

In Strange Bedfellows (1995) Graham McVeigh meets

Columbo & Sgt. Phil Brindle at Crossroad's Cafe - 5610 Fulton Ave, Van Nuys, Los Angeles, California, USA. The building has now been demolished.

## 436

In Dagger of the Mind (1972), only certain location shots and one interior scene (Columbo's visit to Superintendent Durk's gentleman's club) actually were filmed in Britain. The rest of the studio scenes, and all those taking place at Sir Roger's country house, were done in California.

## 437

In Troubled Waters (1975) when Hayden Danziger kills Miss Wells and disposes of the gun in the laundry room, he is locks and unlocks door. But there there is no key in his hand - he is just pretending to turn one.

## 438

The Kosherama restaurant in The Most Dangerous Match (1973) was at 3803 Riverside Dr, Burbank, California, USA. It is now demolished.

## 439

The cosmetic company HQ in The Lovely But Lethal (1973) is at Casa Blanca Poolhouse - 851 Sand Point Road, Carpinteria, California, USA.

## 440

Leo Penn directed three episodes of Columbo: Any Old Port in a Storm (1973), The Conspirators (1978) and Columbo Goes to the Gullotine (1989).

**441**

In Étude in Black (1972) Blythe Danner was about five months pregnant with Gwyneth Paltrow during filming.

**442**

Mrs Columbo, according to Columbo, seems to be a huge fan of every celebrity killer Columbo is pursuing. Or maybe Columbo is just saying that to praise the killer and get them to talk.

**443**

Big Fred's Mansion in A Bird in the Hand...(1992) is at 20181 Northridge Rd, Chatsworth, Los Angeles, California, USA.

**444**

In Double Shock (1973), Columbo helps Dexter in the cooking show, Columbo rolls up his left sleeve, then his right. Half a minute later, Columbo again unbuttons and rolls up his left sleeve.

**445**

Abigail Mitchell's mansion in Try and Catch Me (1977) is located at 880 La Loma Rd., Pasadena, California, USA.

**446**

The Williamson Ranch in Blueprint for Murder (1972) is located at Hidden Valley, California, USA.

**447**

Dean Hargrove wrote the screenplay for four episodes of Columbo: Ransom For a Dead Man (1971), Etude in Black (1972), Candidate for Crime (1973) and Mind Over Mayhem ( 1974). Hargriove (1938-) is a prolific writer and producer creating many shows such as Diagnosis Murder.

**448**

William Shatner on his casting in Columbo:

"I heard that because of my background on Broadway and in regional theater, I had been considered part of the New York acting milieu. Even though I'd lived and worked in Los Angeles for some time, the producers of Columbo considered me a "New York actor," which was a huge compliment."

**449**

There are cases where the murderer is more sympathetic than the victim. For example Ruth Gordon's elderly mystery writer trying to avenge her niece in Try and Catch Me (1977), Janet Leigh's terminally ill and deluded actress in Forgotten Lady (1975), Donald Pleasence's vineyard owner in Any Old Port in a Storm (1973) and Johnny Cash"s singer Swan Song (1974).

**450**

In Publish Or Perish (1974) Columbo says "I'll drink anything."

**451**

The delicatessen and scene of the murder in Fade in to Murder (1976) is located at 3805 Riverside Dr, Burbank, California, USA. The building has since been demolished.

**452**

Oscar Finch's house in Agenda for Murder (1990) is located at 272 Conway Avenue, Los Angeles, California, USA.

**453**

Jackson Gillis (1916-2010) wrote eleven episodes five episodes of Columbo:

Suitable For Framing (1971), Short Fuse (1972), Dagger of the Mind (1972), Requiem For a Falling Star (1973), The Most Dangerous Match (1973), Double Shock (1973), Lovely but Lethal (1973), Troubles Waters (1975), Last Salute To the Commodore (1976), Murder in Malibu (1990), A Bird in the Hand...(1992).

Gillis was a prolific writer of television episodes for over forty years.

**454**

Peter Falk won an Emmy Award for his role in the show's first season: Outstanding Continued Performance by an Actor in a Leading Role in a Dramatic Series - 1972.

**455**

Garland's Jewelry Auction in Death Hits the Jackpot (1991) was held at the Biltmore Hotel - 506 S. Grand Avenue, Downtown, Los Angeles, California, USA.

**456**

On an episode of US chat show The View, Barbara Walters asked Peter Falk what Mrs Columbo was like. He said:

"Well, I knew right from the get-go that we would never see

her, so I didn't waste a lot of time thinking about what she was like".

**457**

The exterior of the ranch house in Negative Reaction (1974) is Greenfield Ranch, 1388 West Potrero Road, Thousand Oaks, California, USA

**458**

The longest episode of Columbo was Forgotten Lady (1975) in Season Five at 1h 40m
.

**459**

Columbo speaks fluent Italian. He has a New York accent and olive complexion and seems Italian-American. In reality, Peter Falk was of Polish-Jewish, Czech-Jewish, and Hungarian-Jewish ancestry and was not an Italian speaker.

**460**

The picnic and basset hound show in Murder, a Self Portrait (1989) was held at Griffith Park - 4730 Crystal Springs Drive, Los Angeles, California, USA.

**461**

Caution: Murder Can Be Hazardous to Your Health (1991) is the longest Columbo title.

**462**

The funeral scene in Columbo Goes to the Guillotine (1989) is set at  Inglewood Park Cemetery - 720 Florence Avenue, Inglewood, California, USA.

## 463

The shortest episodes of Columbo are 70 minutes long.

## 464

The construction site in Blueprint for Murder (1972) is at 1801 Century Park East, Los Angeles, California, USA & Parking Garage next door.

## 465

Oscar Finch's Law Offices in Agenda for Murder (1990) are at 70 N Raymond Ave, Pasadena, California, USA.

## 466

Lauren Staton and Columbo share a dinner in It's All in the Game (1993) at Le Petit Chateau 4615 Lankershim Blvd, North Hollywood, California, USA

## 467

In By Dawn's Early Light (1974) Columbo cannot sleep in the barracks and has to make a telephone call. He gets out of bed barefoot, but the sound of shoes on the floor is heard.

## 468

Louis Jourdan (1921-2015) stars as murderer Paul Gerard in Murder Under Glass (1978). Jourdan started m,making films in Nazi occupied France during World War II and later joined the French Resistance. The suave Jourdan was soon talent spotted by Hollywood and went on to make numerous films and television shows. Two notable roles were in musical Gigi (1958) and as villain Kamal Khan in James Bond film Octopussy (1983).

## 469

Richard Kiley stars as villain  Deputy Commissioner Mark Halperin in A Friend in Deed (1974). Kiley (1922-99). He appeared in many films and tv shows, narrated many documentaries due to his voice and was best known for his work in the theatre, being called  "one of theater's most distinguished and versatile actors."

## 470

Walter Koenig appears as as Sgt. Johnson in Fade in to Murder (1976). Koenig was best known as Checkov in the original Star Trek series. His appearance is an in joke as the murderer in the episode is William Shatner – Captain Kirk from Star Trek.

## 471

Martin Landau as twins Dexter/Norman Paris in Double Shock (1973). Landau (1928 – 2017). He had a long career including in tv series Mission: Impossible (1966 to 1969) and Ed Wood (1994) for which he won as Oscar.

## 472

Janet Leigh stars as Grace Wheeler  in Forgotten Lady (1975). Leigh (1927-2004). In her long career a famous role was in Alfred Hitchcock's Psycho (1960).

## 473

Robert Loggia as Harry Blandford appears in Now You See Him...(1976). Loggia (1930-2015). The charismatic Loggia had many great film roles and numerous appearances in tv episodes.

## 474

Myrna Loy appears as Lizzy Fielding in Étude in Black (1972). Loy had a long career starting in silent movies.

## 475

Season Nine of Columbo had six episodes.

## 476

In Caution: Murder Can Be Hazardous to Your Health (1991)The damage sustained by Wade's car is rusty when shown up close, making it look like old damage rather than new damage.

## 477

Besides being – In Forgotten Lady (1975) Columbo inform us that his wife is "a terrific dancer, and a very good singer."

## 478

Rue McClanahan appears as as Verity Chandler In Ashes to Ashes (1998). McClanahan (1934-2010) was an actress and comedian. Her most notable role was as Blanche Devereaux on The Golden Girls (1985–92).

**479**

Season Six of Columbo has three episodes.

**480**

The ranch house in Strange Bedfellows (1995) is located at 700 West Potrero, Thousand Oaks, California, USA.

**481**

In Murder Smoke and Mirrors (1989) Columbo has a black and white ice cream soda which contains vanilla ice cream, chocolate syrup, club soda, whipped cream and a cherry on top.

**482**

The bookshop in The Conspirators (1978) is located at Hunter's Books, 1002 Westwood Blvd, Los Angeles, California, USA.

**483**

Columbo Goes to the Guillotine (1989) the photographs used for the psychic reading test are of City Hall - 100 N. Garfield Avenue, Pasadena, California, USA, 3500 W. Olive Ave., Burbank, California, USA, Colorado Street Bridge, Pasadena, California, USA and Capitol Records - 1750 N. Vine Street, Hollywood, Los Angeles, California, USA.

**484**

In Grand Deceptions (1989) Columbo says of his wife: "She's a neat housekeeper -- she keeps house like a sergeant major."

**485**

Wagner's house in The Most Crucial Game (1972) is at 944 Airole Way, Bel Air, Los Angeles, California, USA.

**486**

Season Seven has five episodes.

**487**

Levinson and Link originally adapted Columbo into the stage play Prescription: Murder which was first performed at the Curran Theatre in San Francisco on January 2, 1962. Oscar-winning character actor Thomas Mitchell in the role of Columbo. Mitchell was 70 years old at the time. Joseph Cotten was the murderer and Agnes Moorehead the victim. Sadly Thomas Mitchell died of cancer while the play was touring.

**488**

The song being sung by Santini's daughter's boyfriend at the start of the show is the theme song for Charade (1963).

**489**

Barsini's house in Murder, a Self Portrait (1989) is at 24436 Malibu Road, Malibu, California, USA.

**490**

The character of Columbo was created by the writing team of Richard Levinson and William Link. Columbo was partially inspired by Fyodor Dostoevsky's Crime and Punishment character Porfiry Petrovich and G. K. Chesterton's humble priest detective Father Brown. Another influence us Inspector

Fichet from the French suspense-thriller film Les Diaboliques (1955).

## 491

The murder in Identity Crisis (1975) takes place at Santa Monica Pier, Santa Monica, California, USA.

## 492

John Cassavetes co-directed Etude in Black (1972).

## 493

Ricardo Montalbán plays murderer Luís Montoya in A Matter of Honor (1976). Montalban (1920-2009). Mexican Montalban had a long distinguished career in many genres. A charming and distinctive actor, a notable role was as villain Khan in Star Trek II: The Wrath of Khan (1982).

## 494

Season Eight has four episodes.

## 495

Ian McShane appears as Leland St. John in Rest in Peace, Mrs. Columbo (1990) in sadly a minor role. English actor McShane has had a long career (1942-); a famous role was in western tv series Deadwood (2004).

## 497

Lauren Staton's house  in It's All in the Game (1993) is at 23590 Park South St, Calabasas, California, USA.

**498**

Donald Pleasence plays murderer Adrian Carsini in Any Old Port in a Storm (1973). Pleasance (1919-1995). Wonderful iconic actor who also appeared in many cult films. A notable role was as psychiatrist Dr. Samuel Loomis in the Halloween horror firm series.

**499**

The outdoor restaurant where Columbo and Paul Gerard meet) Murder Under Glass (1978) is atCastaway Burbank, 1250 E Harvard Rd, Burbank, California, USA.

**500**

In A Trace of Murder (1997) Columbo offers someone a banana at the murder scene and they take a bite. In the next scene the banana is uneaten.

**501**

Clive Revill plays murderer Joe Devlin in The Conspirators (1978). New Zealander Revill (1930-) has had many film and television roles often in eccentric or foreign roles. He is a noted voice actor, and has spent much of his career on stage.

**502**

David Niven was considered for the role of Paul Galesko in Negative Reaction (1974).

**503**

Matthew Rhys stars as murderer Justin Price in Columbo Likes the Nightlife (2003). Rhys (1974-) is a Welsh actor who has had many good roles during his career including tv spy drama the Americans (2013–2018).

## 504

Gena Rowlands plays Elizabeth Van Wick in Playback (1975). Rowlands (1930-) is a legendary actress who has appearing in numerous film and tv roles. Two famous roles were in the films he Americans (2013–2018).

## 505

Martin Sheen as Karl Lessing (Episode: Lovely but Lethal)

## 506

In Publish or Perish (1974) Riley Greenleaf's house is at 355 S. Mapleton Drive, Holmby Hills, Los Angeles, California, US. It is now demolished.

## 507

Dean Stockwell stars as murder victim Eric Wagner in The Most Crucial Game (1972) and as Lloyd Harrington in Troubled Waters (1975). Stockwell (1936-2021) had a long career starting out as child actor. He appeared in many cult shows such as Quantum Leap (1989–1993). A notable film role was in Married to the Mob (1988).

## 508

Rip Torn plays murderer Leon Lamarr in Death Hits the Jackpot (1991). The distinctive Torn (1931 – 2019) had a long career; famous roles include as Zed in the Men in Black films and as Artie in spoof chat show comedy The Larry Sanders Show.

**509**

Dick Van Dyke plays murderer Paul Galesko in Negative Reaction (1974). Van Dyke (1925-) is a very popular and successful actor, comedian and entertainer. A famous film role was in musical Mary Poppins (1964),

**510**

In Murder in Malibu (1990) Columbo and Wayne are interview the neighbours along the beach and the elderly lady is addressed as Mrs. Shannon. But in the credits the Mrs Shannon actress Louise Fitch is listed as playing Mrs. Gompertz.

**511**

Oskar Werner appears as murderer Harold Van Wick Playback (1975). Werner (1923-1984).Distinctive looking Austrian actor has many film and stage roles such as the film Fahrenheit 451 (1966).

**512**

Nicol Williamson stars as murderer Dr. Eric Mason in How To Dial A Murder (1978).

**513**

Patrick Williams received two Emmy nominations for Outstanding Music Composition for a Series in 1978 (Try and Catch Me and 1989 Murder, Smoke and Shadows.

**514**

In Murder in Malibu (1990) Columbo reviews a tape in Jess

McCurdy's office. He has a plaster on a finger on his right hand. The next moment it is gone.

## 515

In 2010, the Columboplay Prescription: Murder was revived for a tour of the United Kingdom with Dirk Benedict and later John Guerrasio playing Columbo.

## 516

William Link, the co-creator of the series, wrote a collection of Columbo short stories. The Columbo Collection was published in May 2010 by Crippen & Landru.

## 517

Columbo was appeared in novels published between 1994 and 1999 by Forge Books They were written by William Harrington.

## 518

Kens Franklin's house in Murder by the Book (1971) is at 944 Airole Way, Bel Air, Los Angeles, California, USA. It was demolished in 2010.

## 519

The exterior to the Milo Janus building in An Exercise in Fatality (1975) is at 15720 Ventura Blvd, Los Angeles, California, USA.

**520**

The television company building in Make Me a Perfect Murder (1978) is the Lew R. Wasserman building, 1280 Main Street, Universal City, California, USA/

**521**

The stadium exteriors in The Most Crucial Game (1972) are at the Los Angeles Memorial Coliseum - 3911 S. Figueroa Street, Exposition Park, Los Angeles, California, USA.

**522**

Steven Spielberg attended a support event for The Rose Theatre also attended by Peter Falk and many other Columbo cast members. He said he was "grateful for the help Columbo had on his career."

**523**

Steven Spielberg paid tribute to William Link, the co-creator of Columbo in 2020.

"Bill's truly good nature always inspired me to do good work for a man who, along with Dick Levinson, was a huge part of what became my own personal film school on the Universal lot. Bill was one of my favorite and most patient teachers and, more than anything, I learned so much from him about the true anatomy of a plot.

I caught a huge break when Bill and Dick trusted a young, inexperienced director to do the first episode of Columbo. That job helped convince the studio to let me do Duel, and with all that followed I owe Bill so very, very much. My thoughts are with Margery and his entire family."

**524**

After Steven Spielberg who directed Murder By The Book Peter Falk told the show's producers, "This guy is too good for Columbo."

**525**

Falk appeared in character as Columbo in a 1978 episode of The Dean Martin Celebrity Roast making fun of Dean Martin.

**526**

Peter Falk's first lead in a television series was in CBS's The Trials of O'Brien. The show ran from 1965 to 1966, for 22 episodes. Falk is a Shakespeare-quoting lawyer who defends clients while solving mysteries.

**527**

When Peter Falk directed Blueprint For Murder (1972) he asked Steven Spielberg for tips on direction:

"The opening of that show had to do with shooting from sidewalk-level down into this huge hole, and from the huge hole back up, and I wasn't quite certain how to do that. Spielberg had already shot his Columbo. He was nice enough to come on a Saturday morning and give me a few pointers as to the best place to put the camera."

**528**

Stephen Bochco wrote Columbo's Season 1 episode 1 Murder by the Book (1971) at the age of 27."

**529**

Stephen Bochco said Columbo co-creator William Levinson had just one note for Bochco when he joined the Columbo writing staff:

"Peter Falk is Columbo. You don't have to write all of [those quirks], because that's Peter. If you write that stuff, and then Peter does what you're writing on top of being Peter, it's over-the-top. So you want to really underwrite this character, because Peter is so quirky."

**530**

Peter Falk read the Columbo scripts and come up with all the eccentricities onscreen such his strange hand gestures, squinting, strange eating habits and so forth.

**531**

Writer Stephen Bochco received a nice gesture from Peter Falk that Bochco credits with launching his own career:

"In that first year when [Peter Falk] was nominated for Best Actor at the Emmys, he won. And when he went up, he made this wonderful speech in which among other things, he thanked me by name and it really sort of put me on the map."

**532**

Columbo with Peter Falk was first introduced in two television movies on NBC that were a one-off TV-Movie-of-the-Week: Prescription: Murder (1968) has Columbo against a psychiatrist played by Gene Barry. NBC requested that another pilot for a potential series be made to see if the character could be sustained. Another tv movie was made in 1971: Ransom for a Dead Man; Lee Grant played the killer. Falk did not want a weekly series after his unhappy time on tv show The Trials of O'Brien, NBC suggested that Columbo could be in a series with other detective shows and not on every week and agreed to take the part of Columbo.


**533**

Stephen J. Cannell had Robert Culp in mind when he wrote Double Exposure (1973). Culp played the part of the murderer


**534**

In Ashes to Ashes (1998), Columbo says diamonds do not burn. But they do at 850C/1562F.


**535**

Richard Quine (1920-1989) directed three episodes of Columbo: Requiem for a Falling Star (1973), Dagger of the Mind (1972) and Double Exposure (1973). Quine performed on radio, film and stage as a child. Notable films directed include Bell, Book and Candle (1958) and Paris When It Sizzles (1964).


**536**

Columbo originally aired in an NBC Mystery Movie series with other mystery/detective shows. The opening credits depicted a shadowy figure carrying a flashlight slowly walking toward the camera in a desert landscape under dark red clouds. Images of the shows in the series appeared on screen and announcer introduced the evening's episode – for example "tonight, starring Peter Falk as Columbo."

**537**

In Double Exposure (1973) Columbo refers to a previous case for the first time. When he arrives at the crime scene, he said he missed his dinner as he was "working late on the Hayward case" - from the previous episode Candidate for Crime (1973).

He mentions the The Hayward case again in the next episode Publish or Perish (1974).

**538**

A 2008 episode of The Simpsons titled Dial 'N' for Nerder had a reference to the NBC Mystery Movie opening sequence at the end of the episode. The voice over said the series featured Nelson Muntz as Columbo, Dr. Hibbert as Quincy, Rich Texan as McCloud and Mr. Burns and Smithers as McMillan and Wife.

**539**

Patrick McGoohan's last on screen appearance was in the 1998' Columbo episode Ashes to Ashes.

**540**

In Patrick McGoohan's cult spy tv series The Prisoner McGoohan's character Number Six often says "Be seeing you" instead of Goodbye. He uses the line in the spy themed 1975 Columbo episode Identity Crisis."

**541**

In Identity Crisis (1975) Patrick McGoohan's character walks through the amusement park wearing a similar dark jacket with white trim that he wore in The Prisoner.

**542**

Peter Falk had this to say about Patrick McGoohan:

"The first time I ever heard the words "Pat McGoohan" came from the mouth of a man named Everett Chambers, the Producer of Columbo. Somewhere around 1973, Everett said, "There is an actor named Pat McGoohan. And there is no other actor in the world who can do for Columbo what this actor can do. You have to use him." I asked, "Who is he?" (I'd never heard of The Prisoner and I'd never seen him act.) And he said, "Just believe what I'm telling you."

## 543

Faye Dunaway's performance as Lauren Staton in It's All in the Game (1993) resulted in her winning the Outstanding Guest Actress in a Drama Series category at the 46th Annual Primetime Emmy Awards on September 11, 1994.

## 544

Peter Falk had this to say about being introduced to Patrick McGoohan:

"I will be eternally grateful to Everett for that. And what that meant not only to me, but to the show. That was really one of the great moments in the history of the Columbo show. When Everett Chambers said those two words: Pat McGoohan."

## 545

Peter Falk on Patrick McGoohan:

"Patrick and I first met on the plane trip we took to South Carolina to film the show. He was sitting in the back and I was sitting in the front, so we couldn't talk at that point. We took off and made a stop some place, and we were in the waiting room. I don't think we spent three seconds with introductions, or whether we even said "Hello," before the subject of the script was brought up. And, in a very brief exchange, it was agreed that there would be further discussion. That was our first meeting."

## 546

Peter Falk on Patrick McGoohan:

"I remember him saying very early upon our arrival in Charleston...There was something about the man that I was talking to that told me he knew what he was talking about. And I felt so confident about what he could do that without hesitation I said, "Yes." I didn't even know him yet."

## 547

Peter Falk on Patrick McGoohan:

I also remember the first time I walked on the set, and we started rehearsing. I was so aware of the presence of this other actor. He commanded your attention. He was formidable. You were vividly aware of him. That turns an ordinary encounter into something electric. Something that has tension.."

## 548

Peter Falk on Patrick McGoohan:

"There is a scene in Identity Crisis that I now use as a model for the writers who want to work with us... It's an imaginative cat-and-mouse scene between myself as Columbo and the villain, as opposed to a heavy-handed, obvious, boring, pretend cat-and-mouse scene. The scene is set in the living room of the villain's mansion.  And while we are talking, he pipes in opera music, Madame Butterfly, which turns out to be the favorite music of my wife. He offers me wine and cigars. It's not only extremely entertaining, but it has underlying tension."

**549**

Peter Falk on Patrick McGoohan:

Another scene that I use as a model is the first time that Columbo meets the villain in Identity Crisis. That scene was also written by Pat, and it's the best first-encounter ever written for the series. It's done with an economy of words, yet you feel they are immediately caught up in an invisible strain that connects these two men...Columbo has a photograph of a man that he believes is Brenner,..I go to this hotel, and the man I think may be Brenner is standing at the door of the ballroom. . I have the photo in my hand and go up to the man and look at the photograph, and then look up at him. I haven't said anything yet. I look back and forth between the photograph and the man's face several times very intently.

I love that scene because it is an original conception that is unlike any other first encounter we've had. It captures the style of each man, and the core character and determination of each one in just a few words and seconds of time."

**550**

Peter Falk on Patrick McGoohan:

" He has a way of conceiving a scene so that it is not just a hum-drum cliche where a gumshoe cop goes in and asks a bartender some questions and gets some answers. It becomes a layered scene. It's much more interesting and has an unpredictability about it. You don't know, in the beginning, what Columbo is so interested in. That is the kind of thing that I love about Patrick's writing. He doesn't like boredom. His writing shows this, as does his work as a director."

**551**

"Peter Falk on Patrick McGoohan:

"There is the way that he wrote and directed the scene that introduced Columbo to the murder investigation. We never had a scene in the show like this before! It's at the beach. It's night. Columbo emerges from the shadows. He's back a bit from the camera; you just see the cigar smoke. In the foreground is the body, a photographer, and some people making notes. Columbo is very direct and preemptory; he issues commands. You get the feeling that he doesn't want people trampling around the murder scene and the body...he gets those people out of there. All business. The one person he tells to remain is the detective who's there. And having issued those commands, he walks over, kneels down on the sand next to the body, and the detective is also on the sand next to the body, and then, in a friendly voice, says, "How you doin', Cliff?"

## 552

Peter Falk on Patrick McGoohan:

"In another shot, we had the camera in a place I would never have imagined anyone would put it, and it was very effective. Columbo was at a gas station and didn't have enough money to pay the bill. He's on his knees on the pavement trying to pick up some change he's dropped. Then a car pulls up in the background, and after a second, the gas station attendant walks over to Columbo and hands him a ten-dollar bill, and tells him that the guy in the car thinks he could use it. Columbo goes over to the car and puts his head through the open window on the passenger side to thank the driver, and discovers that it's Brenner. The camera is in the back of the car in such an angle that it shows the back of his head and my face."

## 553

Peter Falk on Patrick McGoohan:

"What is particularly enjoyable for me is the fact that I am much better opposite Pat McGoohan than I am in other Columbos. So it's all very well and good for me to talk about his writing ability. There's a Jewish word, "kvell," that has a very special meaning. "They kvell over the accomplishments of their son or daughter." They beam with pride or pleasure. They're overjoyed! When I look at myself in those scenes, I kvell for me! So my appreciation for Patrick goes beyond what he is doing. I'm quite serious about that."

## 554

Joyce Van Patten appears in two episodes of Columbo: Negative Reaction (1974) where she had a famous role as a Nun at a homeless shelter who mistakes Columbo as a homeless man and tries to give him a new coat and Old Fashioned Murder (1976) where she plays the murderer Ruth Lytton. Van Patten (1934-). She has appeared in many tv series and films such as e The Bad News Bears (1976), St. Elmo's Fire (1985). She was married to Dennis Dugan who played policeman Mac in Last Salute to the Commodore (1976).

## 555

In Negative Reaction (1974) Columbo's appearance leads him to being mistaken for a homeless person. He follows a lead to the St Mathew's Mission, where a kind nun, a Sister of Mercy (Joyce Van Patten), assumes Columbo is a homeless man in need. "You're hungry and tired, I can see that. Oh, that coat… that coat, that coat, that coat." she says and offers him a new coat. When Columbo explains that he is, in fact, a cop, the nun believes he is undercover and in disguise!

## 556

In Negative Reaction (1974) Columbo gives driving instructor Mr. Weekly a life and the instructor finds numerous faults with Columbo's car and driving habits including no seat belts.

**557**

Peter Falk was warned against taking on the role of Columbo by John Cassavetes because of "TV's one-dimensionality."

**558**

In 1970 Peter Falk's business manager stole $1000,000 off him. Falk decided to take on the role of Columbo in the series as he needed the money.

**559**

By Season 7 of Columbo Peter Falk was making $500,000 an episode.

**560**

A producer on the casting of Oskar Werner for Playback (1974):

"We're gonna lose the actor. Get to the Beverly Hills Hotel and kiss Oskar Werner's ass,"

**561**

68 of Columbo's 69 episodes went over schedule and over budget.

**562**

Peter Falk looked forward to playing Columbo in his old age," "when the character's forgetfulness and other eccentricities might seem normal."

**563**

The Beverly House in Beverly Hills that appears in Death Lends a Hand (1971) was the house used for the famous horse head scene in The Godfather (1972).

**564**

The Enchanted Hill house in Beverly Hills appears in Identity Crisis (1975) and Fade in to Murder (1976) as locations for the murderers' houses This hilltop house was the former home of silent film screenwriter Frances Marion and her husband Fred Thomson. Microsoft billionaire Paul Allen bought the estate and demolished it in 1997.

**565**

A Case of Immunity (1975) was filmed at silent film comedian Harold Lloyd's house - Greenacres mansion 1740 Green Acres Place Beverly Hills.

**566**

For Season 6 of Columbo Peter Falk was earning $300,000 per episode. This doubled to $600,000 per episode when the series returned in 1989.

**567**

An issue of TV Guide from 1974 suggested that there were several Columbo raincoats that were artificially aged to use in the show.

**568**

In 2018 Columbo's raincoat and shows from the 70s series went on auction at Bonhams in New York. They did not sell as the reserve price of $50,000 was no met.

**569**

At an auction at Bonhams in New York in 2018 a Jaroslav Gebr portrait of Janet Leigh as Grace Wheeler, created for Forgotten Lady in 1975, sold for $1375.

**570**

Season 1 episode 1 of Columbo, Murder by the Book, was first shown on 15 September, 1971.

**571**

In Candidate For Crime (1973) Columbo says Mrs Columbo "takes care of Columbo's social life".

**572**

In 2019 British writer and producer of such shows as Sherlock and Doctor Who caused controversy by saying he wanted to make a radical new version of Columbo stating: "My plan was to put Peter Falk to the back of my mind and start again fromthe beginning. Maybe just go madly different." among other comments. But he later clarified that he did not want to "run" Columbo: What I had advocated, during my one meeting about Columbo, was doing the show EXACTLY THE SAME WAY. No change required. Beyond finding a new lead (which, I accept, might be impossible) there's nothing to alter. It's perfect. Much of the writing – especially the early stuff, but throughout – is inhumanly good. Just matching that would be nigh on unachievable, let alone trying to improve on it.

## 573

Murder by the Book (1971) was originally the second episode from the first season to be filmed after Death Lends a Hand. It was seen as the best episode so it was decided to open with it.

## 574

Since 1971 more than 25 countries have shown episodes of Columbo in countries like Japan, France, Iran and Israel.

## 575

Columbo was shown in communist nations in European in the 1970s because the villains were rich and Columbo had a working class persona - so it was perceived as being anti-capitalist.

## 576

In 1975, Japanese Emperor Hirohito visited the US and asked to meet Columbo.

## 577

After Columbo stopped production in 1978 the communist Romanian government feared there would be riots due to the popularity of the show and that they would get the blame Peter Falk recorded a tv announcement in Romanian for the Romanian government to prevent potential riots.

## 578

In the 1970's Peter Falk was visiting Congress for a conference when he was rushed by two men in black outside his limousine. The men were Iranian bodyguards who wanted an autograph.

**579**

The mystery writer B.K. Stevens said "Is Columbo America's Sherlock?

**580**

In Blueprint for Murder (1972) Mr. Markham's secretary asks Columbo if he is a police officer, but he had shown her his badge through the clear glass door of Markham's office.

**581**

Peter Falk noted:

"I remember being very impressed by Sherlock Holmes. He'd show up, and everybody would turn to him for the answer. I thought it was important in Ransom For a Dead Man that no one turn to me for anything. I was just a local. I wanted to be ignored….Nobody wanted to know this guy's opinion. There's a lack of pretension."

**582**

Columbo is said to agree with Sherlock Holmes when Holmes says in A Case of Identity, "It has long been an axiom of mine that the little things are infinitely the most important."

**583**

Jackson Gillis was the most prolific Columbo writer with writing credits on eleven episodes of Columbo.


**584**

Peter S. Fischer wrote many Columbo scripts. He was a big Columbo fan before he was a Columbo writer. He wrote a Columbo script for fun which he showed to poker friend and Columbo writer Steven Bochco who forwarded it to executive producers Dean Hargrove and Roland Kibbee. They recognized in Fischer "someone with a firm grasp on the Columbo formula."


**585**

Writer Peter S. Fischer struggled to think of an ending for A Deadly State of Mind (1975).


**586**

Columbo creators Richard Levinson and William Link actually wrote only two Columbo episodes: the original TV movies, Prescription: Murder (1968), and Death Lends a Hand (1971).


**587**

Death Lends a Hand (1971) is the only Columbo episode apart from the Ed McBain adaptations where there is no premeditated murder.


**588**

The third most credited Columbo writer is Steven Bochco; none of Bochco's Columbo scripts was his work alone with story ideas from someone else.

**589**

Murder by the Book (1971) credited solely to Steven Bochco, was based on a Larry Cohen idea

**590**

Stanley Ralph Ross (wrote the teleplay for Any Old Port in a Storm (1973) and provided the story for Swan Song (1974). He had never watched Columbo before he worked on the show.

Ross (1935-2000) was a writer for many tv shows such as the Batman tv series. He was an actor, and particularly known for his voice work on animated shows such as Super Friends: The Legendary Super Powers Show

**591**

Howard Berk wrote two scripts: By Dawn's Early Light (1974) and The Conspirators (1978).

**592**

Larry Cohen. Cohen receives "Story by" credit for Any Old Port in a Storm (1973), Candidate for Crime (1973) and An Exercise in Fatality (1974) and is credited with the premise for Murder by the Book. His contribution was in the form of two page story outlines.

**593**

Tyne Daly says she had been a Peter Falk fan before being cast as Columbo in two later roles in A Bird in the Hand (1992) and Undercover (1994). Peter Falk was a fan of hers and asked her to be in Columbo.

**594**

When Columbo returned in the 1980s tv had changed and the production costs had gone up.. The show was not able to have a large cast of famous guest stars in one episode.
.

**595**

James Gregory appears in two episodes of Columbo: Short Fuse (1972) as David L. Bucknor and The Most Crucial Game (1972) as Coach Rizzo. Gregory (1911-2002) specialised in tough characters such as businessmen or policemen.

**596**

In The Most Dangerous Match (1973) the Valley Plaza Hotel is located at the Sheraton Universal Hotel - 333 Universal Hollywood Drive, Universal City, California, US.

**597**

The concert venue at the start of Swan Song (1974) is the Universal Amphitheatre, Universal City, California, USA.

**598**

Peter Falk wanted Columbo to be "liberally sprinkled with comic moments."

**599**

Greg Evigan appears in one episode of Columbo as murderer Harold McCain in A Bird in the Hand (1992). Evigan (1953-)

has had a long career in tv, film and stage. A famous early role was in comedy B. J. and the Bear (1979-81).

## 600

The NFL football footage A Bird in the Hand (1992) is from a Canadian Football League game which has different rules. The NFL is strict about letting people use stock footage in tv shows.

## 601

Last Salute to the Commodore (1976) was featured in an article in the British newspaper The Guardian, in an article titled "When good TV goes bad" calling it "truly berserk."

## 602

Columbo disappeared after the 1977–78 season but was not cancelled.  New executives at tv station NBC wanted programmes aimed at younger audiences.

## 603

Peter Falk had a contract on a yearly basis so it was easy for NBC to not make any more Columbo's after 1978.

## 604

In the 70s Columbo attracted big name stars as the murderer who would not normally appear on tv.

## 605

ABC made no more Columbo's after Columbo Likes the Nightlife in 2003 as it did poorly in the ratings and was too expensive to produce more because of production costs and Peter Falk's salary.

## 606

Gene Barry (1919-2009) starred in one episode of Columbo, the 1968 tv movie Prescription: Murder. Charming baritone voiced Barry was a regular on tv shows.

## 607

Columbo creators Richard Levinson and William Link left the show after the first season. They later "expressed dismay at the poor quality of the writing in subsequent seasons."

## 608

It has been said by those who worked in production on the series that it was difficult to find "inventive stories and high quality scripts."

## 609

The Columbo producers found it difficult to attract famous writers as the Columbo formula was too intimidating.

## 610

Steven Bochco said of Columbo:

"Columbo was crisp at 90 minutes; at two hours, it was a bit indulgent and inflated."

**611**

Columbo co-creator Richard Levinson said the show "was one of those once-in-a-lifetime weddings of character and actor."

**612**

Peter Falk was a perfectionist on set asking for multiple takes which lasted into the night.

**613**

Peter Falk's decision to to buy the rights to a pair of 87th Precinct novels by Ed McBain and adapt them for the series was called "one of the most wrongheaded moves in the celebrated history of Columbo."

**614**

The decision to use 87th Precinct novels by Ed McBain for Columbo by Peter Falk was not supported by other Columbo production staff. One person who did support the change was Patrick McGoohan.

**615**

Peter Falk adored "Patrick McGoohan's unpredictability."

**616**

It is said that during Identity Crisis (1975) director Patrick McGoohan was "drinking heavily" and the episode "incurred substantial overtime costs during production."

**617**

It is said that director Patrick McGoohan's strange decisions and arrogant manner alienated everyone on Identity Crisis (1975) except Peter Falk.

**618**

Even though he was only acting or directing several episodes, Patrick McGoohan was consulted by Peter Falk on many Columbo episodes on casting, scripts and other matters.

**619**

It has been written that Patrick McGoohan "seemed most intent on stretching the Columbo character in new directions. He didn't believe that Columbo was really humble or polite. To him, that was an act, which the detective could turn on or off as the situation merited."

**620**

It has been said of Columbo that "the appeal of the character stemmed from the idea that a genuine bumbler could also be a brilliant puzzle-solver—the "smartest guy in any room. To audiences, that's what made Columbo so fascinating."

**621**

The Rolls Royce was a high status car and symbol of old money in the 70s driven by the rich. As a result the rich murderers of Columbo often drove one or were chauffeured.

The Silver Cloud was the main model from 1966 to 1966. Bentley was a Rolls Royce company and the car is similar to a Silver Cloud.

Columbo appearances:

Etude in Black (1972): Orchestra conductor Alex Benedict's second car is a gold coloured Silver Cloud II in which his wife picks him up from the mechanics.

Dagger of the Mind (1972): Murder victim victim, Sir Roger Haversham, has a green Bentley S2.

Negative Reaction (1974): Murderer Paul Galesko drives a Rolls Royce Silver Cloud III.

Forgotten Lady (1975): Grace Wheeler is chauffeured in a Bentley S1.

How To Dial a Murder (1978): Dr Eric Mason drives a golden 1962 Rolls Royce Silver Cloud III.

## 622

The Stutz Blackhawk was a luxury car made from 1971 to 1987. It was an American designed, Italian built body on a General Motors platform that featured a 24K gold plated trim, maple wood trim and drinks cabinet. It was very popular with entertainers. Elvis bought the first one and at least three more. Lucille Ball, Sammy Davis Jr, Evel Knievel and Elton John were among the many celebrity owners.

In 1971 it cost $22,500, which is equivalent to about $150,000 today.

Only 500-600 models were made

The car appears in:

Forgotten Lady (1975): Grace Wheeler's dance partner Ned Diamond drives a Stutz Blackhawk which we only see through a window looking out onto her driveway.

Murder Under Glass (1978): Restaurant critic Paul Gerard

drives a black and silver model.

## 623

The Mercedes-Benz 280 SE was produced from 1967 to 1972 for the American market. A full-sized 4-door luxury car. A convertible model costs a low six figures. The 280 SE is the car of two different murderers who transport their victim's body in the trunk:

Murder by the Book (1971): murderer Ken Franklin drives a 1968 Mercedes 280 SE convertible.

Blueprint for Murder (1972): architect Elliot Markham drives a 1968 Mercedes 280 SE convertible - the same car used in Murder by the Book (1971).

A Stitch in Crime (1973): heart surgeon Dr Mayfield drives what looks like a gray hardtop model, although we don't get a good look at it.

## 624

The Rolls Royce was a high status car and symbol of old money in the 70s driven by the rich. As a result the rich murderers of Columbo often drove one or were chauffeured.

The Silver Shadow was produced from 1965 to 1980. It was a more modern Rolls Royce, smaller and more suited to American and European roads. Yet offering increased interior space due to unibody construction gave it more interior space.

In 1977 it was renamed Silver Shadow II because of engineering changes. The Silver Shadow has the largest production volume of any other Rolls Royce model.

Any Old Port in a Storm (1973): murderer Adrian Carsini drives a gray 1966 Rolls Royce Silver Shadow with personalized CARSINI plates.

An Exercise in Fatality (1974): health spa franchise owner and murderer Milo Janus drives a red model.

Try and Catch Me (1977): the 2-door version of the Silver Shadow is called a Corniche. Mystery writer and murderer Abigail Mitchell owns a blue model which Columbo drives at one point.

## 625

Jaguar XK120

In The Conspirators (1978) Irish terrorist gun runner Joe Devlin drives a 1952 Jaguar XK 120 Roadster.

## 626

The famous British sports car, the Morgan +4 was produced from 1950 1969.

In Dagger of the Mind (1972) murderer Nicholas Frame drives a +4 (containing the dead body of Sir Roger Haversham) from London to his country estate.

## 627

In Identity Crisis (1975) CIA agent Nelson Bremer drives a very green Citroen SM. This was a luxury car from Citroen and only 2400 models were sold in North America.

## 628

The Ferrari 330 designation encompasses a series of V12 cars produced between 1963 and 1968. It was made between 1966 and 1968 and only 100 were made. Today the car is worth about $2 million.

The car appears in two episodes:

In Double Shock (1973) murderer Dexter Paris drives a 330 GTS before the murder.

In Any Old Port in a Storm (1973) murder victim, Ric Carsini, drives a Ferrari 330 GTS, which has a different license plate to the car in Double Shock.


## 629

Unofficially known as the Ferrari Daytona, the 365 GTB was produced from 1968 to 1973. The car driven by Don Johnson in 80s cop tv show Miami Vice. Today you can buy one for $500,000.

The car is driven in two episodes:

In Lady in Waiting (1971) Beth Chadwick shoots her overbearing brother and only a few days later a blue Ferrari 365 GTB Daytona is delivered to her home.

In Short Fuse (1972) murderer Roger Stanford drives a silver/blue one.


## 630

Thee Jaguar E-type has long been considered a classic British sports car. Produced by Jaguar Cars Ltd from 1961 to 1975, the Jaguar is an E-Type for most of the world but in America it is designated XK-E.

Columbo appearances:

Etude in Black (1972): Alex Benedict drives a silver Jaguar XK-E.

The Greenhouse Jungle (1972) :a yellow Jaguar XKE is pushed into a canyon as part of a fake kidnapping plot.

Requiem for a Falling Star (1973): a blue XK-E is torched by the murderer.

## 631

In 01 to mark the 50$^{th}$ anniversary of the first season of Columbo starting  50 prints of the original Columbo painting from Murder: A Self Portrait (1989) were put on sale.  The paintings by Jaroslav Gebr sold for $250.

## 632

Columbo creator William Link sued NBCUniversal in the 2010s over 40 years of unpaid Columbo royalties. The court awarded Link and the heirs of co creator Richard Levinson $70 million in 2019 but the ward was overturned. A new trial is expected.

## 633

Columbo had this to say about Patrick McGoohan's work on Agenda for Murder (1990):

"When I think about Pat's writing and directing, I think about a scene in the hotel ballroom. Again, one of my all-time favorite scenes. Very rarely in television will you find the director place the camera up near the ceiling of a huge ballroom and encompass an area that is so big you might have a bullfight in it. And these two tiny figures walk in and out of light. Then there's the contrast when you go from that great height, and come down in close. Patrick is wonderful in terms of contrast. Fast and slow. Light and dark. Loud and soft. All those things he manages to combine in the way the scene is conceived. The way it's written, shot, and cropped.

We haven't had a scene in Columbo  like that before or since."

**634**

Columbo had this to say about Patrick McGoohan:

"There's one thing that Patrick can't stand: boring. He's not boring in person. He's not boring when he acts. He's not boring when he writes. And he's not boring when he directs. There's always an imagination and a vitality; there's always contrasts; there's always unpredictability. It's always atmospheric. Patrick has a curious mind, a roving mind. That's why he's wonderful: he's all those things."

**635**

Columbo had this to say about Patrick McGoohan:

As far as why the two of us get along together, I don't know what Pat responds to, but I identify with his sensibility. I admire it. What Patrick feels is funny, I feel is funny. What Patrick feels is dramatic, I feel is dramatic. What Patrick feels is too long, or unnecessary, or too obvious, I feel the same."

**636**

In Publish or Perish (1974) the camera pans up the high rise where Riley Greenleaf's office is located. The real building is the Bank of America's HQ in San Francisco.

**637**

In Blueprint for Murder (1972) Murder Elliot Markham forces Bo Williamson out of his car at gunpoint. Williamson reverses his car and the sound of tires on pavement is heard: but the car is on the grass.

**638**

In Murder by the Book (1971) Columbo makes Joanna Ferris an omelet. He says: "I'll tell you what the secret is to a good omelet -- no eggs, just milk." She laughs at Columbo's mistake.

In the original script, the line is: "The secret is just eggs, no milk."

**639**

In Publish or Perish (1974)  there are discrepancies regarding the car driven by Greenleaf. In the initial scenes, specifically the encounter between Greenleaf and Eddie, as well as the staged parking lot accident, Greenleaf is seen driving a 1969 Cadillac Coupe de Ville convertible. However, at his residence, when Columbo gazes out of a window at the car in the driveway, it inexplicably changes to a 1967 model. Interestingly, when they later step outside for Columbo to inspect the accident damage, the car reverts back to the original 1969 version.

**640**

In Candidate for Crime (1973) the boom mic is seen above Columbo's head when he talks to Nelson about buying a new jacket.

**641**

In Lovely But Lethal (1973), there's a scene where a woman perceives a doctor wearing rubber gloves from her viewpoint. However, when he touches her face from his perspective, he isn't wearing any gloves. Then, from her perspective again, the gloves magically reappear.

**642**

In Suitable for Framing (1971) the boom mic is visible at 5 min 30 seconds. Dale Kingston answers the door and the shadow of the boom microphone moves on the door.

**643**

In Any Old Port in a Storm (1973) Columbo calls from the winery telephone and dials directly, but a sign immediately above it says to dial 3 for an outside line.

**644**

In A Stitch in Crime (1973) Columbo walks through the zoo to meet Harry Alexander and background voices and sounds repeat several times as they are on a tape-loop.

**645**

In Candidate for Crime (1973) Columbo is stopped for a vehicle inspection, and asks several times for directions to Ridgeway Driver", but when the officer gives him directions, it's to "Ridgewood".

**646**

In Double Shock (1973) during the cooking show, Dexter Paris says there are 4 eggs for the recipe. But they break 9 eggs. Dexter puts in 1 and Columbo puts in 8 more.

**647**

In Double Shock (1973)  when walking away from the bank vault, Columbo calls Mr. Paris "Mr. Parks".

**648**

In Lovely But Lethal (1973) Viveca's nail polish changes color in closeups, from pink to red.

**649**

In Double Exposure (1973) Columbo rides in the golf cart with Dr. Kepple with no golf clubs on the cart and Dr. Kepple uses the same club for three consecutive shots, including near the green which no golfer would do.

**650**

Milo Janus's house in An Exercise in Fatality (1974) is located at 10301 Strathmore Dr, Westwood, Los Angeles, California, USA.

**651**

In Blueprint for Murder (1972) Markham forces Williamson out of his car at gunpoint and the camera moves up and zooms back. The boom mic can be seen at the start of the shop.

**652**

In Short Fuse (1972) the plastic hair from the spray can sprayed in to Columbo's hair changes from shot to shot.

**653**

In Étude in Black (1972) Alex Benedict conducts the orchestra on the TV broadcast with his baton but does not match the music being heard.

**654**

In Dagger of the Mind (1972)  the pearl which is dropped in the museum lands on carpet but the sound effect is of it hitting a hard floor.

**655**

In Double Exposure (1973) Kepple leaves Columbo in the supermarket and passes a lady wearing red clothes. When he exits the shot shows the lady by him shopping.

**656**

In Any Old Port in a Storm (1973) there are no news van and camera crews to be seen when Ric's body is brought up on a stretcher. Later the news shows footage of the event.

**657**

Chuck McCann (1934-2018) was an American actor, comedian, puppeteer and television host. He was a prolific voice actor for animated children's shows. He presented and appeared in many productions for children. McCann had roles in many tv shows and films. In 1973 he had a memorable role in Columbo as Roger White the projectionist.

**658**

Near the end of Short Fuse (1972) the door on the cable car switches from opened to closed between shots.

**659**

British actor and comedian said of the series on television panel show QI: "Columbo is the greatest television series ever made,".

## 660

Steven Moffat the writer who has worked on shows such as Sherlock and Doctor Who called Columbo his "favourite ever detective show."

## 661

Murder Under Glass in 1978 had Louis Jourdan as the murderer and this was the last time a villain was older than Falk

## 662

It is said of Columbo that the show is about the murderer and the guest is the star. This is why the whodunit is shown at the start.

## 663

Peter Falk said of Columbo: "He looks like a flood victim. You feel sorry for him. He appears to be seeing nothing, but he's seeing everything. Underneath his dishevelment, a good mind is at work."

## 664

The Most Crucial Came (1972) was first aired on 4 March 1973. Guest star murderer Laurence Harvey sadly died of stomach cancer on 25 November 1973.

**665**

A final episode of Columbo was never made. It was to be called Columbo's Last Case. It opens with the Lieutenant's retirement bash. Columbo was leaving the force.

**666**

In It's All In The Game (1993)  Columbo mentions that the longest he ever worked on a case was 9 years and 4 months.

**667**

Peter Falk wrote the screenplay for It's All In The Game (1993), but started writing the episode in 1971. He had an idea inspired by a real life story from a detective friend who had fallen in love with a suspect.

**668**

Peter Falk decided to heed the producer's advice to hire Patrick McGoohan for By Dawn's Early Light (1974). He said: "If you believe that much in this man, talk to him."

**669**

Faye Dunway won the Outstanding Guest Actress in a Drama Series category at the 46th Annual Primetime Emmy Awards on September 11, 1994 for her role in It's All In The Game (1993).

**670**

Etude in Black (1972) was the first episode of the Columbo series with a longer 90 minutes plus running time. This was over 2 hours with ads. NBC wanted longer episodes to get more ad revenue.

Season 1 episodes ran for about 75 minutes each (90 minutes with ads)

## 671

Because the seventies Columbo series adopted a longer running time, some scenes had to be padded out so there would be enough footage for the running time. For example waiting for the computer printout in An Exercise in Fatality (1974).

## 672

Etude in Black (1972) was shown as a 75 minute version in Canada before the final 91 minute version was shown in the US.

## 673

In Prescription Murder (1968) Columbo's catchphrase "Just one more thing" is "Oh, oh, one more thing before I forget."

## 674

In Prescription Murder (1968) there is a painting of houses on a hill in the reception room of murder Dr. Ray Flemming's office. The same painting is lifted off awall by murderer Dale Kingston in Suitable for Framing (1971).

## 675

A malapropism is "the usually unintentionally humorous misuse or distortion of a word or phrase." Columbo frequently uses malapropisms.

**676**

Robert Butler directed several episodes of Columbo. He said he enjoyed the experience but Peter Falk had lots of control over direction. Butler joked he hoped "to direct a Columbo one day!"

**677**

Columbo often does not immediately introduce himself as a police detective allowing people to think he is no one of importance. He then surprises them by showing them his police badge.

**678**

Milo Janus the exercise expert villain in An Exercise in Fatality(1974) is based on Jack LaLanne. LaLanne (1914-2011) was fitness and nutritional expert and motivational speaker with his own US tv show. He wrote many books. In 1936 he opened one of America's first gym and health clubs.

**679**

Talk radio host Fielding Chase from Butterfly in Shades of Gray (1994) is based on Rush Limbaugh. Limbaugh (1951-2021) was a Conservative political commentator with his own radio and tv show. He often made controversial statements on his shows.

**680**

Max Dyson, the murder victim from Columbo Goes to the Guillotine (1989) is based on James Randi. Randi (1928-2020) was a magician who debunked psychics.

**681**

Dr. Bart Keppel is based on real-life market researcher and subliminal advertising researcher James Vicary. Vicary (1915-1977) invented the concept of subliminal advertising in 1957.

**682**

Rest In Peace, Mrs. Columbo (1990) is the only episode to feature voice-over narrated flashbacks.

**683**

In By Dawn's Early Light (1974) Columbo reveals he went steady with a girl named Theresa in In high school. He gave her a bracelet as a present and years later she told Columbo she still had it. Columbo of course married another woman – Mrs Columbo.

**684**

In Dagger of the Mind (1972) during a montage of Colombo and Chief Supt. Durk on a boat traveling under Tower Bridge, the camera pans from Peter Falk revealing a white microphone.

**685**

Columbo enjoys cooking. He cooks in several episodes and suggests he cooks a lot at home. In his service in the Korean War he was on kitchen patrol.

**686**

The city night scenes in The Greenhouse Jungle (1972) were filmed in Westchester, Los Angeles, California, USA.

**687**

The Redman house in Columbo Goes to College (1990) is at Beach House, 23740 Malibu Rd, Malibu, California, USA.

**688**

The car dealership in Death Hits the Jackpot (1991) is at 15800 Ventura Blvd, Encino, Los Angeles, California, USA.

**689**

In Columbo Likes the Nightlife (2003) Justin and Vanessa meet at the Swingers Diner - 8020 Beverly Boulevard, Los Angeles, California, US.

**690**

In No Time To Die (1990) Columbo says his wedding reception was held at an Italian restaurant. He and Mrs Columbo danced to "Vinnie Scavelli and His Paisanos". MrsColumbo was "as light as a moonbeam. "

**691**

In Dagger of the Mind (1972) Lilian Stanhope calls Columbo 'Loo- tenant' (the American pronunciation) and 'Left-tenant' (the British way). An English actress would use the British pronunciation.

**692**

In Publish or Perish (1974) Greenleaf's publishing company is located in Los Angeles but a cover letter is addressed to him in New York City.

**693**

In Dagger of the Mind (1972) Durk says Sherlock holmes was Scotland Yard's most famous detective. But Sherlock Holmes worked independently of the police.

**694**

In Columbo and the Murder of a Rock Star (1991) the gardener parks his truck at 2406 La Mesa Drive, Santa Monica, California, US.

**695**

In Lady in Waiting (1971) when talking about the new blue car a microphone is reflected in the car's windscreen.

**696**

In Any Old Port in a Storm (1973) Adrian Carsini emerges from the wine cellar after moving the body bare-handed. Then as he runs across to his brother's car, he is leather driving gloves.

**697**

In Mind Over Mayhem (1974) the home garage laboratory has chemical containers with the formula written on them incorrectly.

**698**

In The Conspirators (1978) the radio interviews with the villain Joe Devlin were filed at the KGIL radio station at San Fernando, California, USA

**699**

In An Exercise In Fatality (1974) Columbo says: "before coffee, I'm up and walking around but I'm not awake!"

**700**

In the 1980's Mark Dawidziak wrote a Columbo book called The Columbo Phile: A Casebook for which he interviewed the stars and crew of Columbo.

**701**

In A Case of Immunity (1975) the close up of Habib's license shows it was issued on 1/2/1974 and his birth date as 1918. This would make him 56 years old. His height is listed at 5'8 feet. Sal Mineo, who played Rahman, was only 36 years old at the time and 5'6 feet tall.

**702**

In A Friend in Deed (1974) the helicopter seen on the night patrol switches between two different models – a Bell 206 Jet Ranger and a Hughes 369.

**703**

Mark Dawidziak wrote a Columbo guide called The Columbo Phile in 1989. As a result he became friends with Peter Falk and Falk would consult him on episodes and ask whether a plot device, for example, had been used before.

**704**

The later Columbo's from when the series returned in 1989 had lesser stars overall per episode as the costs of tv had gone up. In the 1970 Columbo one episode would have several famous guest stars in the supporting cast.

## 705

It is said of Peter Falk that he had too much power over the production of Columbo, especially as the series went on. An executive producer with some power would have been a positive thing.

## 706

Peter Falk used two Ed McBain 87th Precinct books for Columbo episodes - No Time to Die (1992) and Undercover (1994).

They are considered to be the among the worst Columbo episodes by fans. Falk used the books after someone told him Ed McBain was the best mystery writer around.

## 707

In A Stitch in Crime (1973) Dr Simpson listens to a patients with the ear pieces on his stethoscope back to front.

## 708

In Playback (1975) the tape outline of the body does not match the position of the body when shown during the murder.

## 709

In Negative Reaction (1974) Columbo is asked to careful when first looking at the ransom note and photo as forensics have yet to analyses it. But he handles it with his bare hands.

**710**

In A Case of Immunity (1975) when Columbo is discussing the murder scene of the Security Chief with Hassan Salah, he says there was no sign of a struggle. But the opening scene showed Rachman Habib overturning chairs, furniture and other items in the room.

**711**

In Columbo Goes to College (1990) Columbo meets the murderers at a bar which is the Carriage Inn - 5525 Sepulveda Blvd, Sherman Oaks, Los Angeles, California, USA.

**712**

In Ashes to Ashes (1998) Liz Houston's house is at 714 West Potrero Road, Hidden Valley, Westlake Village, California, USA.

**713**

Alvin Descler's motel in Negative Reaction (1974) is the Sierra Pelona Motel - 12117 Sierra Highway, Santa Clarita, California, USA.

**714**

In Death lends A Hand (1971) Columbo is called "very observant". "That's not what my wife says" he replies.(1972)

**715**

In Dagger of the Mind (1972) the interiors for the airport, theatre, pub and wax museum were at  Universal Studios, Stages, Universal City, Los Angeles, California, USA.

**716**

In A Stitch in Crime (1973) when Columbo first visits Dr. Mayfield in his office his hair is untidy. When they leave the office and talk again in the hall, Columbo's hair is back to normal.

**717**

In Identity Crisis (1975) when Brenner pours himself and Columbo wine at Brenner's house, he fills the glasses about a quarter full. In the next shot both glasses are almost full.

**718**

In A Friend in Deed (1974) Margaret is pulled out of the pool, and face of the stuntman in her clothes can clearly be seen

**719**

In A Stitch in Crime (1973) the surgeon and nurse remove their masks and hats before their gloves after the first surgery. Gloves are the first piece of equipment to be removed.

**720**

Columbo meets Zeke at the burger stand in Undercover (1994) at 5072 Lankershim Blvd, North Hollywood, Los Angeles, California, USA.

**721**

The western film stet Columbo visits in How to Dial a Murder (1978) is located at Colonial Street, Backlot, Universal Studios - 100 Universal City Plaza, Universal City, California, USA.

**722**

In Dead Weight (1971) Helen Stewart reports the murder on Balboa Island, Newport Beach, California, US.

**723**

The Commodore's residence in Last Salute to the Commodore (1976) is located at 928 Via Lido Nord, Newport Beach, California, USA

**724**

Prescription Murder (1968) was first shown in Hungary in November 1972.

**725**

Murder by the Book (1971) was first shown in Great Britain in 1974.

**726**

The architecture class in Blueprint for Murder (1972) was taught at the California Institute of Technology, 1200 E. California Boulevard, Pasadena, California, USA

**727**

In Candidate for Crime (1973) the tailor tells Columbo that there are many shades of brown, for instance, pale brown, tan, and cream. Cream is not brown. Any painter knows that to obtain cream, one must mix white and yellow. Cream is simply an off-white color. A tailor would be aware of this fact.

**728**

In Last Salute to the Commodore (1976) Charles Clay's yaacht is located at  Balboa Bay Club, 1221 West Coast Highway, Newport Beach, California, USA.

**729**

In Try and Catch Me(1977) Columbo speaks at a book event at the Riviera Country Club, 1250 Capri Drive, Pacific Palisades, California, USA.

**730**

In Blueprint for Murder (1972) Bo Williamson's gold Cadillac is seen to have silver revolvers on the door handles. But in the long shots of the car at the construction site the guns are missing from the car.

**731**

It seems odd that Columbo is a detective with one eye as he would not have joined the police with one eye. If he lost an eye while in the police force he would be working in an office job for the police.

**732**

It is said Columbo is influenced by the character of investigator Porfiry Petrovich from  the 19th century Russian novel Crime and Punishment by Fyodor Dostoevsky. Especially from this quote:

"Porfiry Petrovich piped up once more. 'Just one more tiny question (I know I'm being a nuisance, sir!), just one little idea I wanted to air, purely so as not to forget it later…'"

**733**

Columbo was praised for using mature women in the series who are sometimes forgotten on television and film.

**734**

Ruth Gordon, who played Abigail Mitchel in Try and Catch Me (1977) is the oldest Columbo murderer.

**735**

Janet Leigh was only 48 at the time Forgotten Lady (1975) was filmed. Her character Grace Wheeler is much older in the episode.

**736**

Kim Hunter plays Aunt Edna in Suitable For Framing (1971). Aunt Edna is much older than Hunter was when the episode was filmed.

**737**

In 2017 on Peter Falks birthday 16 September, a special art exhibition celebrating the Women of Columbo was staged. Tika Viker-Bloss exhibited her paintings at The Shop in north London. The paitings are of some of the women who appeared in Columbo, murderesses and other characters.

Viker-Bloss says she was watching Columbo on DVD and paused the episode and noticed a striking image of Vivian Dimitri from Rest in Peace, Mrs Columbo (1993). She took a photo of the image and used it as a basis for a painting. She used this method for all her paintings.

**738**

In 2017 a biography of Peter Falk  called Beyond Columbo: The Life and Times of Peter Falk written by Richard A. Lertzman and William J. Birnes. It has lots of material about Columbo and interviews with  Dabney Coleman, Ed Begley Jr, ,Steven Spielberg and other cast and crew members from the series.


**739**

Theresa Goren's beach house in Murder in Malibu (1990) is at 33148 Pacific Coast Highway, Malibu, California, USA


**740**

The top ten Columbo episodes on imdb.com (Internet Movie Database) are

1. Any Old Port in a Storm (1973) 8.2

2. Try and Catch Me (1977)8.2

3. A Friend in Deed (1974)  8.1

4. Now You See Him (1976) 8.1

5. Swan Song (1974) 8

6. A Stitch in Crime (1973)  7.9

7. Negative Reaction (1974) 7.9

8. Forgotten Lady (1975) 7.9

9.  Double Exposure (1973) 7.8

10.  By Dawn's Early Light (1974)  7.8

**741**

The first Columbo pilot Prescription: Murder (1968) was a ratings success. But Peter Falk and the producers were busy so it was three years before the next Columbo was made.

**742**

The cinematographer for Murder by the Book (1971) was Russell Metty – who had won an Oscar working on Stanley Kubrick's Spartacus.

**743**

Romanian communist dictator Nicolae Ceausescu feared social unrest when the Columbo came to an end in 1978 because of the popularity of the series.

**744**

The Columbo series in the seventies won two Golden Globes and ten Emmy awards.

**745**

The Greenhouse Jungle (1972)was first shown in Italy in September 1979.

**746**

Columbo was very popular in Iran in the 1970s. Famous dubbing actor Manouchehr Esmaeili dubbed Peter Falk into Persian.

**747**

In the opening scene of Any Old Port in a Storm (1973)the four wine experts hold their glass correctly but fail to swirl and smell the wine before drinking it.

**748**

The Mayfield house in A Stitch in Crime (1973) is at
944 Airole Way, Bel Air, Los Angeles, California, USA

**749**

In Lovely But Lethal (1973) Shirley Blaine's obituary lists her as Shirley Blane, but she is  credited as "Shirley Blaine."

**750**

In Swan Song (1974) there is an almost zero possibility of Tommy's parachute landing near the scene of the crash site as the plane continued flying after Tommy jumped out.

**751**

In An Exercise in Fatality
When Columbo arrives at Milo's house, he initially is talking to him through a closed glass door, yet his voice can be heard clearly.

**752**

In Double Exposure (1973) the golf course is located at
Scholl Canyon Golf & Tennis Club - 3800 E. Glenoaks Blvd. Glendale, California, USA.

**753**

When Rosanna Wells is singing the song Volare In Troubled Waters (1975) and hands out the microphone to a member of audience, it does not have any effect on the sound of her voice - it sounds the same with or without the microphone.

**754**

In Double Exposure (1974) when Dr. Kepple offers Vic some beluga caviar, he pronounces it as "be-lu-jah" instead of "be-lu-ga"

**755**

In A Bird in the Hand... (1992) Harold <cCain's house is located at Kelly Gulch - 1801 N. Topanga Canyon Boulevard, Topanga, California, USA.

**756**

The funeral in Ransom for a Dead Man (1971) was held at the Hollywood Forever Cemetery - 6000 Santa Monica Blvd., Hollywood, Los Angeles, California, USA.

**757**

In Sex and the Married Detective (1989) Dr Joan Allenby stops off at The Frolic Room cocktail lounge at 6245 Hollywood Blvd, Los Angeles, California, USA

**758**

In Make Me a Perfect Murder (1978) Mark McAndrews's beach house is located at 26646 Latigo Shore Drive, Malibu, California, USA.

**759**

In Lovely But Lethal (1973)  Viveca's beauty mark is originally on her right cheek, but it switches back and forth between her left and right cheeks several times at the start of the episode.

**760**

In Publish or Perish (1974) Columbo reveals that he and his wife enjoy Bette Davis movies and enjoy watching them at 2 am in the morning.

**761**

In A Case of Immunity (1975) Columbo reveals his wife buys pottery at The Farmers Market similar to an Arabian-style urn in the episode.

**762**

In Rest In Peace, Mrs Columbo (1990) Columbo reveals his wife loves marmalade.

**763**

In Prescription: Murder (1968) Columbo says that every morning his wife gives him a pencil and every day he loses it.

**764**

The airport in Ransom for a Dead Man (1971) is Burbank Airport, Burbank, California, USA.

**765**

Columbo meets the insurance representative in Murder by the Book (1971) at Tail o' the Pup - 311 N La Cienega Blvd, Los Angeles, California, USA.

**766**

In Death Lends a Hand (1971) Columbo gets pulled over by a cop and escorted down a street. The street is 4100 block of Lankershim Boulevard, Studio City, California, USA.

**767**

Columbo has a chat with a gold pro in Death Lends a Hand (1971) at Hansen Dam Golf Course - 10400 Glenoaks Blvd., Pacoima, Los Angeles, California, US.

**768**

The exterior of the Brimmer Associates building in Death Lends a Hand (1971) is located at 15720 Ventura Blvd, Los Angeles, California, USA.

**769**

The exterior of Mitilda's Art Gallery in Suitable for Framing (1971) is located at 653 N. La Cienega Boulevard, West Hollywood, California, USA

**770**

Aunt Edna's house in Suitable for Framing (1971) is located at 1240 Stone Canyon Road, Los Angeles, California, USA.

**771**

The Chadwick mansion in Lady in Waiting (1971) is at 1155 Oak Grove Av San Marino, CA 91108, USA.

**772**

The car crash investigation scenes in Short Fuse (1972) are at Mount San Jacinto, California, USA.

**773**

The auto repair shop in Étude in Black (1972) was at 14540 Erwin St, Van Nuys, Los Angeles, California, USA. It has been demolished.

**774**

Rosanna Huffman plays Tracy O'Connor in Suitable for Framing (1971). She was married to Columbo creator Richard Levinson.

**775**

The gas station in The Greenhouse Jungle (1972) is at 8610 S Sepulveda Blvd., Westchester, Los Angeles, California, USA.

**776**

The marina in The Greenhouse Jungle (1972) is at Marina del Rey, California, USA.

**777**

When Columbo is cooking on Dexter's tv cooking show in Double Shock (1973) the amount of lemon juice in the glass keeps changing. One person tried the recipe from the episode and said there was too much lemon juice!

**778**

The Colonial Mansion owned by Jarvis Goodland in The Greenhouse Jungle (1972) was located at the Backlot, Universal Studios - 100 Universal City Plaza, Universal City, California, USA. It was demolished in 2005.

**779**

Columbo meets Dobbs at the Ocean Side East Cafe in The Most Crucial Game (1972) at 401 Santa Monica Pier, Santa Monica, California, USA. It is now the Mariasol restaurant.

**780**

The grocery store in Double Exposure (1973) was GEMCO, 11051 Victory Blvd., North Hollywood, Los Angeles, California, US. It closed in 1986.

**781**

In Double Exposure (1973) one detective tells Columbo there are only two entry points for the murderer. Another detective tells Columbo the building is large and there are many entry points for the killer.

**782**

In Double Exposure (1973) when Columbo meets Kepple in

the grocery store he has four of Kepple's books. Later he has five books.

**783**

In Double Exposure (1973) when Dr Kepple starts the tape recording in the theatre the recorder is on play already and he presses stop.

**784**

In Double Exposure (1973) when Dr Kepple is outside Mrs Norris's house a microphone can be seen in the car window.

**785**

In Publish or Perish (1974) Columbo drinks from a red plastic cup before the manuscript service arrives. In the next scones the cup has gone.

**786**

In Swan Song (1974) Columbo tells Tommy he can here a difference between two musical arrangements of I Saw the Light – one featured a murdered girl who was a soprano, the second for a new girl who is a contralto. But a contralto is lower than a soprano and the voices are the wrong way round.

**787**

In An Exercise in Fatality (1974) Columbo puts down his pencil on Janus's desk and the sound effect is heard in the next shot.

**788**

In 2013 TV Guide magazine included Columbo on a list of The 60 Greatest Dramas of All Time.

**789**

Columbo creators Richard and William Link said: We recalled a meeting with Peter Falk after the series had established itself as a hit. He had just returned from New York, and we informed him that we were leaving the show. He was genuinely distressed and urged us to stay. Surprised, we reminded him that the three of us were in constant conflict. We had kept him away from dailies, we had hidden scripts, we had even ordered the editors to lock their doors to him. Why on earth would he want us to continue on for the second season? Falk smiled. "Because now," he said, "I trust you."

**790**

Columbo inspired a series of cop shows with cops who were slightly eccentric characters – such as Kojak, Cannon, Barnaby Jones and Baretta.

**791**

When appearing in play The Prisoner of Second Avenue Peter Falk complained that backstage visitors were not interested in complained that no one visited his dressing room to discuss the play; all they wanted to talk about was Lieutenant Columbo.

**792**

Cecil Smith, the television columnist praised the Columbo scripts: "the brightest dialogue and most intricate plots around."

**793**

When studio executives tried to influence Peter Falk about the show he would get angry and talk about "the Universal assembly line." At the time Universal would churn out tv shows.

**794**

A number of unique videotape releases of Columbo were available in Japan with distinctive covers.

**795**

A laser disc edition of Columbo was released only in Japan. There are 6 volumes with the whole set consisting of 26 episodes. They were only released in Japan and are collectors' items.

**796**

Most of the Columbo novels have been adapted into novels in Japan. First editions go for high prices.

**797**

Columbo was dubbed initially by Asao Koike in Japan. He is said to have a more intellegent and youthful voice for Columbo rather than the English deep one.

Koike sadly died in 1985 and Taro Ishida took over Columbo dubbing duties imitating the style of Koike.

**798**

Clocks play a big part in Columbo. Murderers commit their

crime within a timeframe and often try to suggest the murder was committed at another time to create a fake alibi. Watches are often broken or doctored to create an alibi.

## 799

In Playback (1975) villain Harold Van Wyck's digital watch was created by Midas Electronics. Harold says to Columbo: "you remember the time better if you see it printed".

## 800

Columbo says he has to write everything down because he has a bad memory.

## 801

In Forgotten Lady (1975) Columbo admits he's rarely in the office down at Homicide "none of the murders take place there, you know."

## 802

In Troubled Waters (1975) and Playback (1975) it is revealed Columbo hates guns, hates the noise and is a terrible shot.

## 803

In Forgotten Lady (1975) it was revealed that Columbo goes 10 years without getting a new photo for his police ID.

## 804

In Try And Catch Me (1977) Columbo says: "I like my

job...Some of the murderers I meet, I even like them too....Not for what they did, but for that part of them which is intelligent, or funny,...or just nice."

## 805

Why Columbo likes working in Homicide: " In Murder, A Self Portrait (1993) Columbo explains why he works in homicide: Why not? It's nice, clean work...Now, the Robbery boys, you won't believe the miserable places they gotta go into..."

## 806

In Columbo Goes To College (1990) Columbo says: "I follow my nose,...and when I get the scent, there's very little that I wouldn't do in order to solve the case."

## 807

In Columbo Goes To College (1990) Columbo gives advice to aspiring detectives: "Don't talk too much...You don't have to blab everything right away....Wait, who knows what will happen...Timing, that's important...And luck!...You gotta be lucky."

## 808

In Forgotten Lady (1975) says "From my experience, I've discovered that people don't usually forget
to do that-which-they-usually-do."

## 809

In The Conspirators (1978) Columbo compares detective style to a pinball game:

"The way I keep steering and pushing and pulling at things, someday the whole sky is gonna light up and say TILT!!!"

## 810

In Double Shock (1993) Columbo reveals "I'm very big on motive."

## 811

In It's All In The Game (1993) Columbo reveals he worked on one case for 9 years and 4 months.

## 812

In How To Dial A Murder (1978) Columbo is asked by the murderer "Do you enjoy games, Lieutenant?" He replies:"I've never had time for them, sir..."

## 813

In the The Bye Bye Sky-High I.Q. Murder Case (1977) it is revealed that Columbo liked model trains. "I tell ya the truth, I could play with something like that
forever."

## 814

In Make Me A Perfect Murder (1978) it is revealed Columbo liked making model aeroplanes: "But I always wrecked 'em before I finished 'em"

## 815

In The Bye Bye Sky-High I.Q. Murder Case (1977) Columbo

says he likes riddles but "doesn't have a feel for 'em"

## 816

In Any Old Port In A Storm, (1973) Columbo says he is "probably the only Italian in the world who can't sing." But he does try.

## 817

Columbo hums "Molly Malone" in Last Salute To The Commodore (1976) and sings ""Swing Low, Sweet Chariot," "Yankee Doodle" and "My Darling Clementine" in Make Me A Perfect Murder (1978). Also sings My Darling Clementine in Murder With To Many Notes (1998).

## 818

Columbo likes to sing while he is alone driving in his car.

## 819

Columbo says he "a little cooking...nothing fancy," and he reads the food columns in Murder Under Glass (1978).

## 820

In How To Dial A Murder (1978) Columbo says he likes playing pool but does not get much time to play.

## 821

In The Greenhouse Jungle (1972) Columbo reveals his father taught him to play pool and that he is sad he does not have room for a pool table in his basement.

**822**

In The Greenhouse Jungle (1972) Columbo says he loves to go to the beach.

**823**

In The Conspirators (1978) Columbo says he likes pinball as it reminds him of his youth playing pinball in the candy store.

**824**

In The Most Crucial Game (1972) Columbo reveals he likes to listen to baseball matches while "testing out a new hammock".

**825**

In By Dawn's Early Light (1974) Columbo says he enjoys the outdoors as he grew up in the city and enjoyed childhood summer camps,

**826**

In Any Old Port In A Storm Columbo says he enjoys taking the "wife and kid" on a picnic.

**827**

In Death Hits The Jackpot (1991) Columbo reveals he pans to take Mrs Columbo camping in the forest for their 25th wedding anniversary.

**828**

Columbo enjoys fishing and in Dead Weight (1971) the owner

of the chilli restaurant offers to give him free chilli for any fish he has caught.

## 829

Columbo a collector, he reveals in Rest In Peace, Mrs Columbo (1990)

## 830

In The Conspirators (1978) Columbo says he learned to play darts from Sgt Gilhooley at the 12<sup>th</sup> Precinct.

## 831

Columbo tries playing quoits on shipboard in Troubled Waters (1975) but noe very well: he throws the quoit straight into the ocean.

## 832

In Last Salute To The Commodore (1976) Columbo says he wants to try transcendental meditation but his legs won't go into the right position.

## 833

Columbo's raincoat was made in Spain by a company called Cortefiel. The company makes designer clothing and since the 1970's only sells its clothes in Europe. So Columbo's raincoat is a designer coat.

## 834

Peter Falk said the script for Prescription: Murder (1968) specified that Columbo wear a raincoat. Columbo's creators, Levinson and Link said Falk was mistaken and that the script called for Columbo to wear an overcoat.

**835**

Perter Falk wore the same coat in the seventies Columbo series. He had three stand in coats and one was auctioned for charity in 1974. It was bought for $1000.

**836**

In 1989 TV Guide magazine wrote an article on the raincoat used for the new episodes of Columbo. The pattern of the original coat was copied and it was aged by soaking it in black tea and running over it with a car.

**837**

Columbo's original raincoat was owned by Peter Falk. "I have a great deal of affection for it," Falk said in 1988. "I take great care of it. I've been known to say I put out a saucer of milk for it every night!" he once said.

**838**

Columbo's raincoat is a short length so would not provide much protection for his legs in the rain.

**839**

The name of the exact model of Columbo's raincoat remains a mystery.

**840**

In one of his Columbo novels, author William Harrington has

Columbo explaining that he always wears the raincoat because it acts as a filing system, allowing Columbo to carry around his daily accumulation of clues related items easily.

## 841

In By Dawn's Early Light, (1975) Columbo wears his coat with a sleeveless white shirt underneath.

## 842

In Candidate For Crime (1973) Columbo reveals "Every once in a while I think about getting a new coat, but there's no rush on that. There's still plenty of wear in this fella!"

## 843

In Troubled Waters (1975) Columbo wears his coat even on a cruise in Mexico.

The ship's captain (Patrick MacNee) asks Columbo:
"Tell me, Lef'tenant,... do you expect inclement weather in the Mexican waters?"
Columbo replies: "No, they tell me the weather's great this time of year!"

## 844

In The Bye Bye Sky-High I.Q. Murder Case (1977) we see Columbo in one of his few appearances without the raincoat when he gets soaked in a thunderstorm! He explains his wife is cleaning the coat.

## 845

In Negative Reaction (1974), Columbo visits a soup kitchen to interview a witness. The Sister of Mercy (Joyce Van Patten) thinks Columbo is homeless because of his coat and offers to replace it. Columbo explains he is a policemen and she praises him for his undercover homeless outfit!

## 846

In Death Hits The Jackpot (1991) Columbo wears his raincoat to a Halloween party and he is praised for his fancy dress outfit as "an eccentric millionaire".

## 847

In Rest In Peace, Mrs Columbo (1990) Columbo puts his raincoat over the murder victim so a woman cannot see the corpse.

## 848

Columbo uses his stop watch when he needs to time something to prove a theory for a case.

## 849

In Make Me A Perfect Murder (1978) gets involved in a police chase and suffers whiplash in a crash. At the time he was singing and trying to adjust his mirror!

## 850

In Matter Of Honor (1976) Columbo is involved in a car accident and his car gets impounded.

**851**

In Caution: Murder Can Be Hazardous To Your Health (1991) Columbo accidentally crashes into the murderers car. But it gives him a chance to find a clue on the killer's car.

**852**

In Old Fashioned Murder (1976) Columbo crashes into the back of a police car at the crime and just says: "sorry about the car"!

**853**

In Negative Reaction (1974) Columbo's driving instructor is appalled to find that Columbo's car has no seat belt. Columbo says: "Is that a requirement, sir? new regulation?"

**854**

In Death Lends A Hand (1971) Columbo gets pulled-over by the police because his car has a broken right turn signal. "It's the second time I got pulled-over today." he says.

**855**

In Uneasy Lies The Crown (1990) Columbo reveals he has never used his siren light for his car because his cigarette lighter used to plug it in does not work.

**856**

In Caution: Murder Can Be Hazardous To Your Health (1991) Columbo reveals his car has no tape deck.

**857**

In Forgotten Lady (1975) Columbo is late for an appointment because his car has broken down on the freeway.

**858**

In A Friend In Deed (1974) Columbo's car breaks down frequently.

**859**

In Candidate For Crime (1973) the police stop Columbo to inspect his car. He fails as his windscreen wiper is broken, an indicator is not working, a light is broken and a door handle has fallen off.

**860**

In Make Me A Perfect Murder (1978) Columbo's can't decide whether to buy a new pair of shoes or a bumper for his car.

**861**

Columbo's Cabriolet Peugeot 403 was available to buy in red, ivory, yellow, metallic blue, metallic green, light grey, metallic dark grey, and black.

**862**

In Sex And The Married Detective (1989) we learn Columbo played the tuba - in high school as it "it was the only instrument they had left".

**863**

In It's All In The Game (1993) Columbo gets a new tie from the murderer played by Faye Dunaway which he wears when he sees her.

**864**

In Troubled Waters (1975) we see Columbo in a tropical shirt.

**865**

In Lady In Waiting (1971) the killer points a gun at Columbo.

**866**

In Butterfly In Shades Of Gray (1994) murderer Fielding Chase attempts to shoot Columbo with a shotgun.

**867**

In Rest In Peace, Mrs Columbo (1990) murdere Helen Shaver attempts to murder Columbo with poisoned marmalde.

**868**

In Columbo Goes To The Guillotine (1989) murderer Elliot Blake tries to kill Columbo with a guillotine.

**869**

In Murder Under Glass (1978) murderer Paul Gerrard tries to kill Columbo with poisoned wine.

**870**

In How To Dial A Murder (1978) the murderer tries to kill Columbo with attack dogs.

**871**

In these episodes that Columbo tempts the killer to plant evidence:

Columbo Goes To College (1990)
Troubled Waters (1975)
A Friend In Deed (1974)

**872**

In these episodes Columbo gets killer's girlfriend/boyfriend to help him solve the case:

Prescription: Murder (1968)
A Trace of Murder (1997)
Undercover (1994)
Lady In Waiting (1971)

**873**

These Columbo episodes have a military person as the murderer.

By Dawn's Early Light (1974)
Grand Deceptions (1989)
Dead Weight (1971)

**874**

In these episodes Columbo used unusual fingerprint evidence.

Suitable For Framing (1971)
Troubled Waters (1975)
Death Hits The Jackpot (1991)

## 875

In these episodes Columbo tricks the murderer into confessing.

A Case Of Immunity (1975)
Rest In Peace, Mrs Columbo (1990)

## 876

Columbo episodes where the killer or accomplice used a disguise are:

Prescription: Murder (1968)
Sex And The Married Detective (1989)
Identity Crisis (1995)
Strange Bedfellows (1995)
Candidate For Crime (1973)
Now You See Him (1976)
Columbo And The Murder Of A Rock Star (1991)
Fade In To Murder (1976)
Last Salute To The Commodore (1976)

## 877

These are the Columbo episodes where the killer uses gadgets to commit the murder:

Columbo Goes To College (1990)
Short Fuse (1972)
Mind Over Mayhem (1974)

**878**

Columbo episodes where the murder was made to look like a natural death:

Double Shock (1973)
Caution: Murder Can Be Hazardous To Your Health (1991)
Uneasy Lies The Crown (1990)

**879**

In these Columbo episode the killer was a doctor or involved in the medical profession:

Prescription: Murder (1968)
A Stitch In Crime (1973)
Sex And The Married Detective (1989)
Double Exposure (1973)
Mind Over Mayhem (1974)
Uneasy Lies The Crown (1990)
A Deadly State Of Mind (195)
How To Dial A Murder (1978)

**880**

In these Columbo episodes the killer is a lawyer:

Ransom For A Dead Man (1971)
Agenda For Murder (1990)
Columbo And The Murder Of A Rock Star (1991)

**881**

In Murder By The Book (1971) the murder is carried out by gunshot at a holiday cabin..

**882**

In Agenda For Murder (1990) Columbo discusses a phone call with Oscar Finch at Biltmore Hotel - 506 S. Grand Avenue, Downtown, Los Angeles, California, USA.

**883**

38 people were killed by shooting in Columbo.

**884**

12 people were killed by bludgeoning in Columbo.

**885**

4 people were strangled in Columbo.

**886**

4 people were killed in a car explosion in Columbo.

**887**

4 people were killed by poisoning in Columbo.

**888**

3 people were killed by drowning in Columbo.

**889**

3 people were killed by a fall in Columbo.

**890**

2 people were killed by electrocution in Columbo.

**891**

2 people were killed by hanging in Columbo.

**892**

2 people were killed in a plane crash in Columbo.

**893**

1 person was killed by a bull in Columbo.

**895**

1 person was killed by killer dogs in Columbo.

**896**

A Stitch In Crime (1973) sees a jar of cold cream as the murder weapon

**897**

Undercover (1994) is the Columbo episode with the most murders: 4.

**898**

Last Salute To The Commodore (1976) sees a microscope as the murder weapon.

**899**

24 females were murdered in Columbo, with 68 males being murdered.

**900**

2 people were murdered by stabbing in Columbo.

**901**

The Sherwin dental practice in Uneasy Lies the Crown (1990) is at 1900 Avenue of the Stars Building - 1900 Avenue of the Stars, Century City, Los Angeles, California, USA.

**902**

In Murder in Malibu (1990) the cafe used for the alibi by the murderer is The Pink Motel & Cadillac Jack's Diner, 9457 San Fernando Road, Sun Valley, California, USA.

**903**

These Columbo episodes had suffocations:

to look like drownings:

Murder, A Self Portrait (1989)
Any Old Port In A Storm (1973)

to look like accidents:

An Exercise In Fatality (1974)

suffocation using a small steel bar to the throat:

Try And Catch Me (1977)

locked in a sound proof vault:

Any Old Port In A Storm (1973)


**904**

These Columbo episodes had murder by poisoning or drugs:

Swan Song (1974)
Murder Under Glass (1978)
Rest In Peace, Mrs Columbo (1990)
Uneasy Lies The Crown (1990)


**905**

In these Columbo episodes murder was committed using animals as weapon:

A Matter Of Honor (1976) (a bull)
How To Dial A Murder (1978) (two Doberman pinschers)


**906**

Columbo's Peugeot 403 car weighed about 2,340 pounds/1061 kg.


**907**

Emmy awards for Columbo include:

1971 -- 1972

1) Outstanding writing achievement in a drama series:
Richard L. Levinson and William Link, Death Lends A Hand, Columbo

2) Outstanding continued performance by an actor in  a

leading role in a dramatic series: Peter Falk, Columbo

1973 -- 1974

Outstanding limited series: Columbo

1974 -- 1975

1 ) Outstanding single performance by a supporting actor in a comedy or drama series (for a onetime appearance in a regular or limited series): Patrick McGoohan, By Dawn's Early Light, Columbo

2) Outstanding lead actor in a limited series: Peter Falk, Columbo

1975 -- 1976

Outstanding lead actor in a drama series: Peter Falk, Columbo

1989 -- 1990

1) Outstanding lead actor in a drama series: Peter Falk, Columbo

2 ) Outstanding guest actor in a drama series: Patrick McGoohan, Agenda For Murder, Columbo

1993 - 1994

Outstanding guest actress in a drama series: Faye Dunaway, It's All In The Game, Columbo

**908**

In Caution: Murder Can Be Hazardous to Your Health (1991) Wade Anders's office is at 434 N Larchmont Blvd, Los Angeles, California, USA.

## 909

A Columbo spin off of sorts called Mrs Columbo was broadcast for 13 episodes between 1979 and 1980. 24 year old Kate Mulgrew starred as Mrs Columbo. She plays Kate Columbo a news reporter.

The Columbo producers and Peter Falk never endorsed the show and the link to Columbo was dropped with the second series being called Kate the Detective/Kate Loves a Mystery.

## 910

Michael Lally's first Columbo appearance was in Murder By The Book (1971) where he played a crime scene cop in the background.

## 911

Candidate For Crime (1973) is the only episode where the murderer whistles. Columbo's theme tune This Old Man.

## 912

These are the lyrics of Columbo's favourite This Old Man tune:

This old man, he played one
He played knick-knack on my thumb
Knick-knack paddywhack, give your dog a bone
This old man came rolling home

This old man, he played two
He played knick-knack on my shoe
Knick-knack paddywhack, give your dog a bone
This old man came rolling home

This old man, he played three

He played knick-knack on my knee
Knick-knack paddywhack, give your dog a bone
This old man came rolling home

This old man, he played four
He played knick-knack on my door
Knick-knack paddywhack, give your dog a bone
This old man came rolling home

This old man, he played five
He played knick-knack on my hive
Knick-knack paddywhack, give your dog a bone
This old man came rolling home

This old man, he played six
He played knick-knack on my sticks
Knick-knack paddywhack, give your dog a bone
This old man came rolling home

This old man, he played seven
He played knick-knack up in heaven
Knick-knack paddywhack, give your dog a bone
This old man came rolling home

This old man, he played eight
He played knick-knack on my gate
Knick-knack paddywhack, give your dog a bone
This old man came rolling home

This old man, he played nine
He played knick-knack on my spine
Knick-knack paddywhack, give your dog a bone
This old man came rolling home

This old man, he played ten
He played knick-knack once again
Knick-knack paddywhack, give your dog a bone
This old man came rolling home
.

**913**

Jonathan Tunick composed the soundtrack for Murder Under Glass (1978). Tunick (1938-) is American orchestrator, musical director, and composer noted for his extensive work in the theatre on such production on those by Stephen Sondheim.

**914**

Gil Melle (1931-2004) was an American composer, jazz musician and artist. In his work composing soundtracks for television he was one of the first composers to use electronic instruments in his work giving his early seventies compositions a distinctive sound. He worked on four Columbo episodes:

Death Lends A Hand (1971)
Dead Weight (1971)
Short Fuse (1972)
Blueprint For Murder (1972)

**915**

Columbo Goes To College (1991) features a student asking Columbo about his work with the FBI in "the Devlin case" which is the name of the IRA gunrunner villain in The Conspirators (1978).

But the student is presumably taking about a different case as the case discussed includes horse racing in the murder.

**916**

An Exercise in Fatality (1974) and Death Lends A Hand (1971) both have the same street scene shown on a monitor.

## 917

The jazz club in Etude In Black (1972) is also used as the basement of the wax museum in Dagger of The Mind (1972).

## 918

Ken Franklin's house in Murder By The Book (1971) was also... used for Eric Wagner's house in The Most Crucial Game (1972).

## 919

Columbo has no distinctive boss or superior mentioned o seen in separate episodes.

## 920

Columbo works alone which would probably not happen in real life given the nature of police work and bureaucracy.

## 921

When on one occasion Columbo is told by assistant Sergeant Wilson that Captain Ritichie says Columbo is a legend in the department, Columbo says:"Captain Ritchie said that?? I wonder why he said that…"

## 922

In 1985 Peter Falk appeeted as a Columbo type character in a series for adverts for Italian supermarket chain COOP. He had a dog and talked about his wife.

Ad #1: Basic spot (Lenght: 45 Seconds)
Ad #2: COOP's products (Lenght: 15 Seconds)

Ad #3: Fruits and vegetables (Lenght: 30 Seconds)
Ad #4: Christmas (Lenght: 33 Seconds)

## 923

In the series Columbo's superiors often give him a younger detective to train. The assistants do not last too long as Columbo likes to work alone.

## 924

France Nuyen who plays Mary Choy in Murder Under Glass (1978) was married to Columbo villain actor Robert culp from 1967-70.

## 925

Writer Robert van Scoyk received an Edgar Allan Poe Award from the Mystery Writers of America for his teleplay for Murder Under Glass (1978).

## 926

The mechanical shark Bruce from Jaws (1975) makes a cameo in Fade in to Murder (1976).

## 927

In Identity Crisis (1975) Columbo is hindered by a spy who knows lots of classified information. He has a visit from the Director of the CIA called Philip Corrigan which is the name of the spy in 1945 serial Secret Agent X-9.

**928**

In Now You See him (1976) Santini is caught by evidence in the carbon ribbon on Jerome's IBM Selectric typewriter which has an imprint of everything typed.

**929**

In Now You See Him (1976) Santini states that he thought he had created the perfect murder. Columbo informs him that a "perfect murder is only an illusion."

**930**

For the role of Negative Reaction (1974) Glenn Ford was asked to play murderer Paul Galesko. He wanted $50,000 to play the part. Dick Van Dyke played the role.

**931**

In Last Salute to the Commodore (1976) Columbo does not say "Just one more thing" and "Something's been bothering me".

**932**

The outside set of Deschler's hotel room in Negative Reaction (1974) is also the set of Psycho (1960).

**933**

Vera Miles who plays murderer Viveca Scott in Lovely But Lethal (1973) appears in Psycho (1960). Scott says to Columbo that "she couldn't hurt a fly". Murderer Norman Bates says the same line in Psycho.

**934**

Peter Falk said that one of his favourite scenes was the one where Columbo is invited on stage to take part in The Great Santini's magic act in Now You See him (1976).

**935**

Columbo Cries Wolf (1990) has see Columbo solve a murder in the fastest time – in 24 hours.

**936**

Lee J. Cobb was considered for the role of Columbo. Cobb (1911-1976) had a long distinguished career in film, television and on Broadway.

**937**

In Forgotten Lady (1975) Columbo is asked why he is never in the homicide office at police headquarters. He says : "Well, I don't get down there too much. None of the murders take place there, you know?"

**938**

Columbo's Peugeot 403 was already old when the series started as it was stopped being made in 1966.

**939**

The title of A Bird in the Hand...(1992) comes from the proverb that A bird in the hand is worth two in the bush: it is better to hold onto something you have rather than risk it trying to get sonmething better.

**940**

Peter Falk decided to return Columbo in 1989 after an 11 year absence by a $600000 per episode wage and an Executive Producer role.

**941**

Actor and comedian Don Rickles was considered for the role of Alvin Deschler in Negative Reaction (1974). In the end the role went to Don Gordon.

**942**

In Candidate for Crime ( 1973) Columbo is asked by a policeman if he would consider getting another car? Columbo replied: "I've got another car. My wife drives it. But that's nothing special   just transportation."

**943**

Arthur, the vendor of Columbo's one of Columbo's hot dog stands in Griffith Park, Los Angeles notes that Columbo "likes his hot dogs charred".

**944**

Dick Van Dyke was cast as the murderer in Negative Reaction (1974) only a few days before filming commenced. Van Dyke had recently moved away from his comedy roles with a well received part as an alcoholic in the television drama The Morning After (1974).

**945**

A helicopter sequence of ashes being scattered over the

Hollywood sign in Los Angeles was filmed in Ashes to Ashes (1998). Dumping ashes on the sign is illegal, but creative license allowed it.

## 946

Walter Koenig, Chekov in Star Trek appears as Seargeant Johnson in Fade In To Murder (1976) . The murderer in the episode is played by William Shatner, Captain Kirk in Star Trek.

## 947

In Identity Crisis (1975) Columbo and Brenner go into a nearby room where Brenner pulls out a small address-book type notepad and writes in it. In the next shot, the small notebook in Brenner's hands is now a full-sized group of papers.

## 948

Forgotten Lady (1975) was the first episode in which the first Columbo appeared in a tuxedo.

## 949

In 1984 CBS wanted to bring Columbo back in a new mystery wheel tv series alongside Kojak.

## 950

Peter Falk stated: "It's obvious that people like seeing the murderers bite the dust."

**951**

Sorrell Booke, best known as southern Boss Hogg in The Dukes of Hazzard, plays a member of a MENSA-type organization in The Bye-Bye Sky High I.Q. Murder Case(1977) and Swan Song (1974). Booke (1930-1994) played was highly trained and appeared in many roles and worked as a voice actor. He spoke 12 languages.

**952**

Ginger Rogers and Fred Astaire were considered for roles in Forgotten Lady (1975).

**953**

Anthony Hopkins was asked to appear in Last Salute to the Commodore (1976) but said no.

**954**

Peter Falk believed that an actor is responsible for finding and putting together his own costume.

**955**

In 2010 the Columbo stage play Prescription: Murder was revived for a tour of the United Kingdom with Dirk Benedict and later John Guerrasio as Columbo.

**956**

Falk appeared in character as Columbo in 1977 at The Dean Martin Celebrity Roast of Frank Sinatra.

**957**

In 2021 The Gebr Art Estate offered prints of Blue Horse from the episode Suitable For Framing  (1971). They retailed for $160.

**958**

Peter Falk said Columbo's main characteristics were indicated in the script but he added some personal touches.

**959**

Columbo appears 16 minutes into Murder by the Book (1971)

**960**

Jeffrey Cava wrote the screenplay for Murder With Too Many Notes (2000); it is his only writing credit.

**961**

64 year-old cinematographer Russell L Metty's wanted noir style lighting for Murder by The Book (1971) and argued with director Steven Spielberg and the producers. He got his way with the lighting for the episode but a brighter look was adopted for later episodes in the first season.

**962**

Murder by the Book was May to June 1971 and went over its 12 day shooting schedule.

**963**

Steven Spieberg was going to direct an episode of Columbo when it was going to return in 1988. But a writers' strike meant he could not fit it into his schedule and Columbo returned in 1989.

**964**

Between 1968 and 2003 Columbo won 13 Primetime Emmy awards from 39 nominations.

**965**

The year with the most Columbo episodes was 1973 where eight new ones were shown.

**966**

Columbo creators Richard Levinson and William Link had work on shows such as Mannix and The Psychiatrist so had to bring in other people to write Columbo scripts.

**967**

In Murder by the Book (1971) murderer Ken Franklin drives a 1968 Mercedes 280 SE convertible with a 'Have A Nice Day' bumper sticker.

**968**

No Time To Die was the title of a Columbo episode in 1992. It was also the title of a James Bond movie in 2021.

**969**

Columbo's raincoat is single breasted and has five buttons.

**970**

Columbo's raincoat has two pockets which are invariably open as he uses them a lot.

**971**

Columbo's raincoat is almost like a superhero costume. When he is wearing a new coat in Now You See Him (1976) he struggles to think without his old coat.

**972**

Columbo stores food and drink in his raincoat including hard boiled eggs, a thermos of coffee, a salt shaker, raisins, gumdrops and other items including dog biscuits.

**973**

There is a theory that the raincoat work in Prescription: Murder in 1968 is different from the one used subsequently as it seems longer.

**974**

Peter Falk says he bought his coat in New York: "In 1966..., I was walking on 57th Street in New York when it started to rain. I entered a shop and bought a raincoat. When I had to find one for Columbo, I simply took this one."

**975**

Freddy Brower's apartment in Death Hits the Jackpot (1991) is located at the Nate Starkman & Son Building - 544 Mateo St, Los Angeles, California, USA.

**976**

In Undercover (1994) Columbo stays undercover at at the Vincent Arms hotel which is Cameo Hotel - 504 S Bonnie Brae St, Los Angeles, California, USA.

**977**

In Murder Under Glass (1978) murderer Paul Gerard prepares poison from a blowfish but his latex gloves keep disappearing and reappearing from scene to scene.

**978**

The Conspirators script was intended as a pilot for another series but adapted for a Columbo episode.

**979**

In Make Me a Perfect Murder (1978) Columbo is shown how to change reels of tape; but he was shown how to do this in Double Exposure (1973)

**980**

In Make Me a Perfect Murder Columbo meets the murderer Kay Capstone at a boarded up house.

**981**

In Make Me a Perfect Murder (1978) Columbo appears before and during the murder. This house is from the set of disaster movie Eathquake (1974/)

**982**

Just One More Thing is the title of Falk's autobiography

**983**

Peter Falk won three Emmy wards for Columbo and said at the 1972 Emmy Awards: "I'm trying to figure out some way to appear humble."

**984**

Columbo's specialty is making an omelette, he reveals in Murder By The Book (1971).

**985**

In Matter Of Honor (1976) Columbo gets in trouble in Mexico after a car accident. But the police know Columbo from the case in Troubled Waters (1975) (involving a Mexican cruise) and let him off.

**986**

In How to Dial a Murder(1978) the dogs lick Columbo's face and peanut butter can be seen on Peter Falk's face which has been used to get the dogs to lick his face.

**987**

In The Conspirators (1978) murderer Joe Devlin drives a Jaguar XK120.

**988**

In The Conspirators (1978) Joe Devlin has three pinball tables in his living room. A 4-Square (a 1971 game by Gottlieb), Flying Carpet (a 1972 Gottlieb) and one which is unknown.

**989**

In Columbo Goes to the Guillotine (1989) Columbo is shown card trick in a magic shop, but we can see the whole deck is made up of aces of diamonds.

**990**

In Agenda for Murder (1990) and Murder in Malibu (1990) the same black BMW 750iL is driven.

**991**

In Death Hits the Jackpot (1991) Freddy Bower bought the lottery ticket on October 2, 1991.

**992**

At the start of It's All in the Game (1993) the water in the fountain outside Lauren Staton's house flows backwards showing that the shot is being payed backwards.

**993**

Columbo often wears a pyjama top underneath his raincoat

when called out to a murder scene during the night.

## 994

British actor and tv presenter Stephen Fry compared Columbo to ancient Greek philosopher Socrates in an episode of tv quiz show QI.

## 995

In The Conspirators (1978) Columbo says  he'd like to have a pinball machine at home but  "the Mrs would never go for it".

## 996

In By Dawn's Early Light, (1975) Columbo goes to the bathroom to have a wash in the morning wearing his coat like a bathrobe.

## 997

In The Bye Bye Sky-High I.Q. Murder Case (1977) Columbo says his wife wants to have the raincoat "cleaned and burned!"

## 998

In It's All in the Game (1993) the dead man blinks when the buzzer goes off.

## 999

In A Trace of Murder (1997) Columbo offers a banana to a colleague at the crime scene and he takes a bite. In the next shot the banana is whole.

**1000**

In A Case Of Immunity (1975)  and No Time To Die  (1992)
Columbo wears a tuxedo with his raincoat.